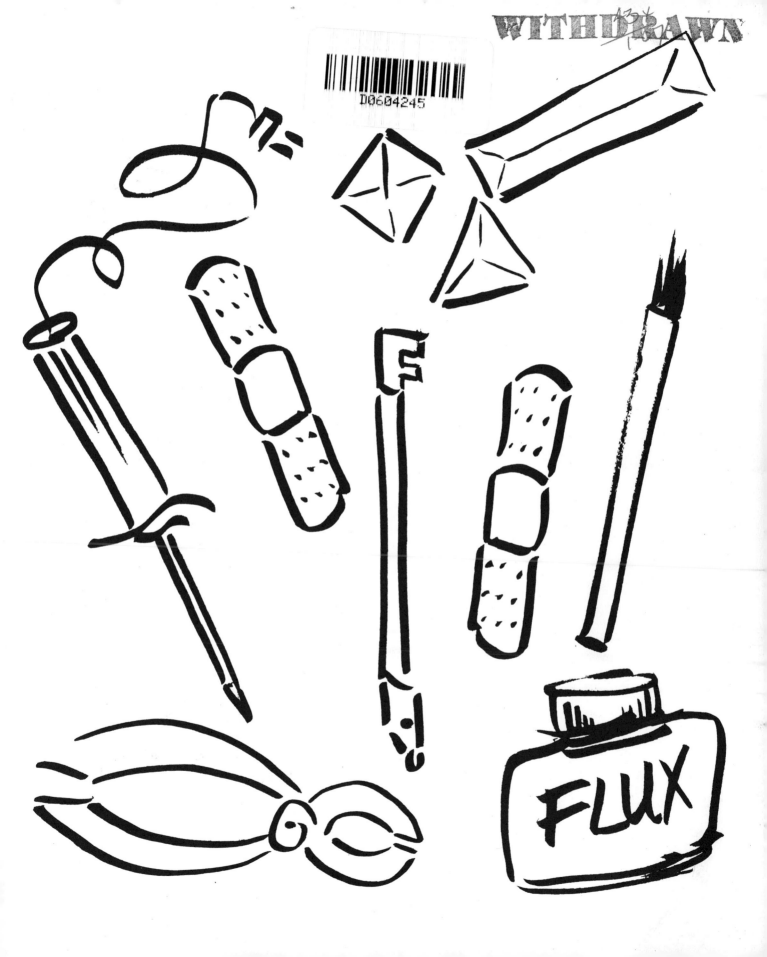

FLUX

Stained Glass
for the first time™

Stained Glass
for the first time™

Art Glass Originals

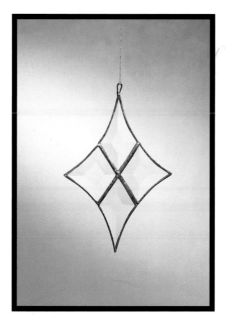

Sterling Publishing Co., Inc.
New York
A Sterling / Chapelle Book

Chapelle:

Jo Packham, Owner

Cathy Sexton, Editor

Staff: Marie Barber, Ann Bear, Areta Bingham, Kass Burchett, Rebecca Christensen, Brenda Doncouse, Dana Durney, Marilyn Goff, Holly Hollingsworth, Susan Jorgensen, Barbara Milburn, Linda Orton, Karmen Quinney, Leslie Ridenour, Cindy Stoeckl, Gina Swapp

Photography: Kevin Dilley for Hazen Imaging, Inc.
Gallery Photography: Various professional photographers unknown by name.

If you have any questions or comments or would like information on specialty products featured in this book, please contact Chapelle, Ltd., Inc., P.O. Box 9252, Ogden, UT 84409 • (801) 621-2777 • (801) 621-2788 Fax • e-mail: Chapelle1@aol.com

Library of Congress Cataloging-in-Publication Data Available

10 9 8 7 6 5 4 3 2 1

Published by Sterling Publishing Company, Inc.
387 Park Avenue South, New York, NY 10016
© 2000 by Chapelle Ltd.
Distributed in Canada by Sterling Publishing
c/o Canadian Manda Group, One Atlantic Avenue, Suite 105
Toronto, Ontario, Canada M6K 3E7
Distributed in Great Britain and Europe by Cassell PLC
Wellington House, 125 Strand, London WC2R 0BB, England
Distributed in Australia by Capricorn Link (Australia) Pty Ltd.
P.O. Box 6651, Baulkham Hills, Business Centre, NSW 2153, Australia
Printed in China.
All Rights Reserved

Sterling ISBN 0-8069-6829-X

About the Authors

While growing up, Jennifer was always involved in some form of art project. As she matured, she used her talent to explore all types of art mediums including drawing, sculpture, and woodcarving. In 1990, Jennifer was hired as an artist for a local art glass studio. She quickly became adept at creating custom stained glass designs and through practice became skilled in stained glass assembly.

When the business was put up for sale, Jennifer and her mother, Leta, saw an opportunity to continue exploring the glass medium and purchased the business. They called their new venture Art Glass Originals. Shortly thereafter, the business became a family affair with the addition of Jennifer's sister RaiChel, who, in addition to designing, is in charge of material management, and their father Robert, who finds time from production to do stained glass repairs and restoration.

Art Glass Originals' creations are featured in residential, commercial, and religious installations in Utah and surrounding western states, and as far away as New York and Hawaii. Art Glass Originals combine sandblasted etching, dimensional glass carving, copper, and wood with the stained glass to create unique works of art. Current plans are underway to include a glass art gallery and gift shop, and future plans include the addition of fused glass creations.

This book is dedicated to Colin,
our son and brother,
who could not be here
to share this with us.

custom designed by Art Glass Originals for Mr. and Mrs. Scoffield

custom designed by Art Glass Originals for Mr. and Mrs. Cody

9

Table of Contents

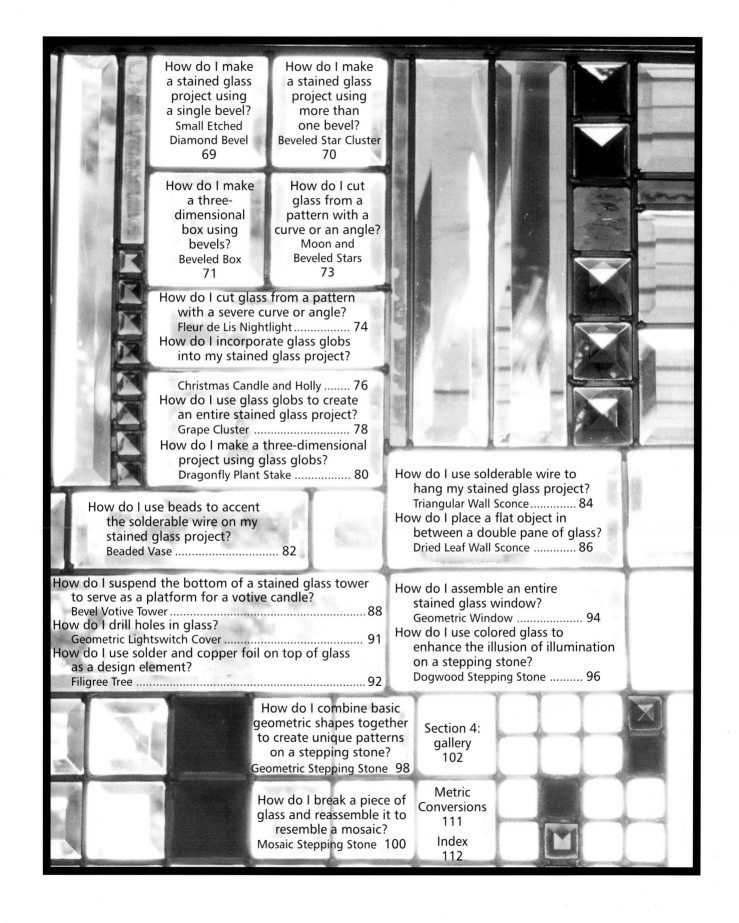

Stained glass for the first time

Introduction

Stained glass was first introduced to the world in the late 11th century. By the 13th century, stained glass windows were very popular in religious applications. That is why today when many people think of stained glass, elaborate cathedral windows come to mind. It wasn't until the early 19th century that nonreligious stained glass in private homes became accepted.

In the early 1800s, Louis Comfort Tiffany, the son of the famous jeweler, made the popularity of stained glass for the home soar. It was he who created the foil technique for stained glass. And although Tiffany was a master craftsman in several fields, he has become best known for his intricately detailed lamps and windows.

In the early 1900s, Frank Lloyd Wright used stained glass in geometric designs. He used rigid metal came to provide strength and straight lines to his designs. Today, prairie lamps closely mimic Wright's geometric creations.

The name "stained glass" originates from the old process of applying additives to molten glass to create a desired color which gave it a painted or stained appearance. Additives were also applied in this way to create small details such as an expressive face or folds in a robe. The present-day method to create these details are still much the same. However, to create solid or swirling colors, the additives are added to the original mixture rather than later. The name "stained glass" represented these procedures and has become a catch-all phrase for leaded, beveled, and colored glass.

The lead bars running through the primeval designs found in churches and cathedrals were merely used for structural support. Today, the lead lines for most stained glass creations has become an integral part of the artistic design, in addition to providing structural support.

custom designed by Art Glass Originals for Mr. and Mrs. Cody

Section 1: *stained glass basics*

How to use this book

For the person who is trying stained glass for the first time, this book provides a comprehensive guide to products, tools, supplies, and techniques that can be used to artistically create stained glass works of art. There are many methods for working with stained glass and for creating stained glass projects, but we have found the methods presented in these pages to be the simplest and most efficient.

Section 1: This section will familiarize you with the stained glass basics, from safety guidelines to tools and supplies. The list of tools and supplies is necessary for creating stained glass projects (shown and detailed on pages 19–23). Additionally, each technique or project gives a list of other items you will need for that specific project. It is assumed that you will have on hand necessary items such as pencils, permanent markers, all-purpose glue, rulers, paper towels, cloths, glass cleaner, etc. In addition, a detailed, step-by-step practice section is included.

Section 2: This section teaches eight simple stained glass techniques that give the basis for creating a myriad of stained glass projects. It is recommended that you work through these techniques before moving on to the projects. The patterns have been provided for your use. Once you become proficient at these techniques and have created a few of the projects, you can move on to more complicated projects. You can make the project larger or smaller, simply by enlarging or reducing the pattern. Keep in mind that the smaller the project, the more difficult it becomes to create because of the cutting and manipulation of the glass pieces.

Section 3: Once you've become skilled at the techniques for creating stained glass projects, select a project that goes beyond the basics. An approximate size is given for each of the projects, but they can be made in any size. Enlarge (or reduce) the pattern for the project to the size you desire and feel free to substitute glass types and/or colors to customize the project to your liking. Keep in mind that you may need to refer back to the practice and/or technique sections.

Section 4: The gallery section presented is a collection of antique and custom stained glass work created by well-known stained glass artisans. It is important that you understand that the purpose of this publication is to teach the simple basics for working with stained glass for the first time. It takes a great deal of practice before one would be able to achieve some of the advanced pieces shown. We included them strictly for your enjoyment and inspiration.

Safety guidelines

- Make certain to wear safety glasses while cutting or grinding glass.

- Make certain to wear latex gloves to prevent flux from coming into contact with the skin.

- Make certain to wear latex gloves to prevent patina from coming into contact with the skin.

- Make certain to wear latex gloves to prevent etching cream from coming into contact with the skin.

- Work in a well-ventilated area as smoke and fumes from the flux are emitted during the soldering process. If natural ventilation is not possible, a fume trap can be purchased at stained glass supply stores.

- When working with lead, make certain to thoroughly wash hands before eating or touching the eyes or mouth.

- Make certain any open wound is bandaged (or wear latex gloves) prior to working with lead.

What terms do I need to know?

Bending came
Measuring a length of came by inserting the edge of the glass piece into the came channel and following the contours. The ends are then marked and any excess is cut off with lead dykes.

Break lines
Any line included on a pattern that runs from the point of a sharp curve or angle. The purpose of these lines are to provide structural support and prevent breakage.

Breaking, running, or tapping
Manipulating the glass to "break" along a score line.

Burnishing
Rubbing the copper foil flat along the edges of the glass.

Foiling
Lining the edges of glass with copper foil.

Grinding
Grinding the edges of glass with a glass grinder to ensure a proper fit.

Melt-through
Solder that "melts through" to the opposite side on any copper foil or came project.

Scoring
Making a "scratch" on the glass with a glass cutter to cause a controlled break.

Soldering
Melting a layer of solder onto copper foil to form a small, even mound which provides structural support.

Stretching came
Stretching lead came before it is placed around the edges of glass.

Tack-soldering
Melting a dot of solder onto all intersecting joints on any copper foil project to prevent movement.

Tapping
Tapping a score line with the ball end of the glass cutter until a fracture line appears. After scoring the glass, before tapping, make certain to turn the glass over.

Thermoshock
Breaking of glass caused by intense heat or cold.

Tinning
Melting a thin layer of solder onto copper foil for decorative purposes only.

It is important for you to know as you read the descriptions and directions in this book that although we have used terms that are common to this endeavor, stained glass terminology may vary from manufacturer to manufacturer and from store to store.

What types of glass can I use?

The basic recipe for clear glass is sand, limestone, potash, and iron. The oldest recipes for making colored glass are still used today. A few examples of the additives to create the various colors are: sugar and sulphur to make amber; dichrome to make green; copper oxides or cobalt to make blue; and selenium, gold, and cadmium to make red, orange, and yellow. Adding gold is why red color ranges are so expensive. Some of these additives can also make the glass more temperamental. No matter how careful one is in making a score or running a score line, some glass will insist on fracturing straight through the middle.

Traditionally made colored glass is most commonly made in England, Germany, and Poland and is available in a seemingly limitless variety of colors and color combinations. This glass is generally more expensive due to the labor involved in the creation process. After a mixture of oxides are combined and heated to a molten state, the glass is mouth-blown into a cylinder. The ends are sliced off, the cylinder is sliced open and laid on its side, then reheated in an oven to allow it to unroll. Traditionally made glass is often uneven in thickness, which is not necessarily a bad thing. Although more difficult to work with, the unevenness can create a richer, more interesting stained glass panel.

Colored glass made in the United States is more automated. Molten glass is poured onto a long table where a heavy roller rolls it into a uniform $1/8"$ thickness. Once flattened, the glass is allowed to cool. This glass is available in a wide variety of colors and textures and is commonly used in mass-produced windows and doors. Because it is of uniform thickness and generally smooth, it is recommended for the beginning stained glass artist.

Textured glass (clear or colored) made in Europe and the United States are made using stamps, textured rollers, or molds to create the many different textures. One very popular textured glass is clear gluechip. Heated glue is poured and smoothed over a piece of etched glass (clear or colored) and is placed in a warm oven. As the glue solidifies, the heat causes it to shrink and pull up thin layers of glass in small sections resembling ice crystals and ice fractures.

Tempered (safety) glass and laminated glass cannot be used when creating stained glass projects because it cannot be cut.

Etched glass will be briefly touched upon in this book. Etching uses an acid or powerful bursts of sand to dissolve or blast away layers of glass.

Mirror is a piece of glass that has been plated with a silver backing. It is made in several thicknesses and can be manipulated the same as any piece of glass, however it is important that the silver backing is not disturbed.

Regardless of the type and color of glass called for in these projects, keep in mind that part of the fun in creating stained glass pieces is selecting the glass you wish to use. Find color combinations that are pleasing, then consider the function of the finished project. Transparent glass, for example, would be a perfect choice for a door opening into a garden, but it wouldn't be a good choice for a bathroom window. In addition, it would be impossible for a stained glass retail outlet to stock all of the different types of glass in all of the available colors. Therefore, be prepared to use your imagination when selecting the type(s) of glass you will ultimately use to create your stained glass masterpiece.

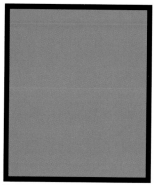

Transparent

Opaque

Clear Gluechip

Colored Gluechip

Transparent Streakie

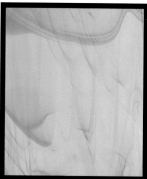

Semi-opaque Streakie

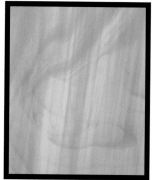

Opaque Streakie

Opaque Iridescent

Waterglass

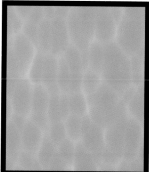

Light Hammer

Transparent Confetti

Opaque Confetti

Clear Stamp

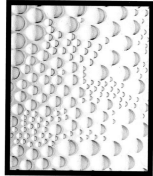

Clear Raindrop

Clear Granite

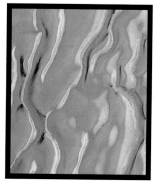

Transparent Ripple

Is there a correct way to lay out pattern pieces on the glass?

When configuring the layout of the pattern pieces for cutting, allow enough room for scoring between each piece. Make certain one score line will not run into another pattern piece. It is also important to lay out the pattern pieces to follow the pattern, if any, of the glass.

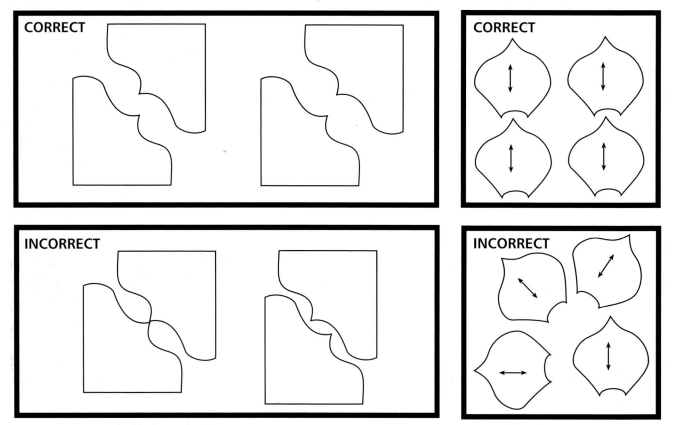

Cutting cannot be done around sharp curves. The dotted lines illustrate the proper way to score a sharp curve and the numbers indicate the scoring and breaking order.

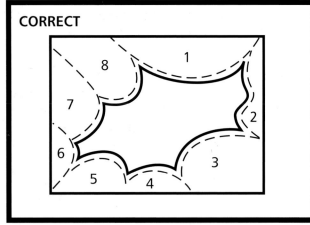

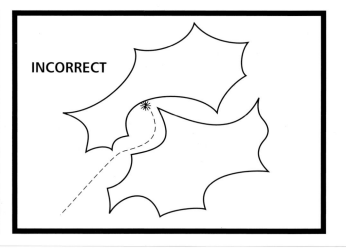

What tools and supplies do I need to get started?

The following list of tools and supplies is necessary for creating stained glass projects. In *addition, each technique or project gives a list of other items you will need for that specific project.*

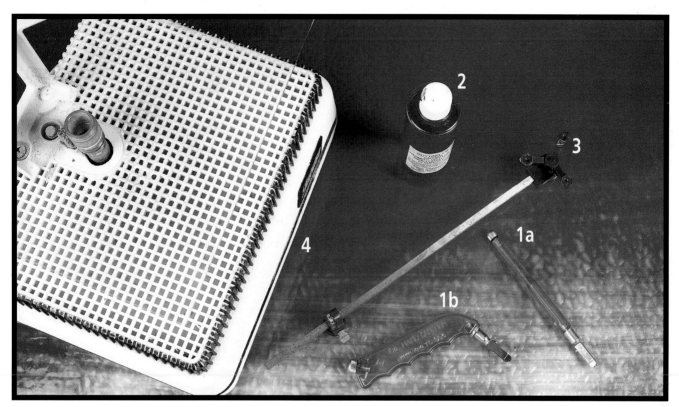

1 Glass Cutter
A glass cutter is used to "score" (scratch) glass in order to cause a controlled breakage. Two styles are shown — 1a is a comfort-grip glass cutter; 1b is a pistol-grip glass cutter.

2 Glass-cutting Oil
Glass-cutting oil is oil that is used along the cutting wheel on a glass cutter to prevent chipping along the "score" (scratch) line.

3 Circle/Strip Cutter
A circle/strip cutter is a tool that enables the "scoring" (scratching) of perfect circles and straight lines on glass.

4 Glass Grinder
A glass grinder is used to grind down the edges of glass pieces to ensure a proper fit. When using copper foil to assemble a stained glass project, a glass grinder can be used to slightly abrade all the edges of each glass piece to ensure the foil will properly adhere to the glass.

5 Grozing Stone (not shown)
A grozing stone is used to abrade the edges of glass primarily for the purpose of applying copper foil. A grinder can be used in place of a grozing stone.

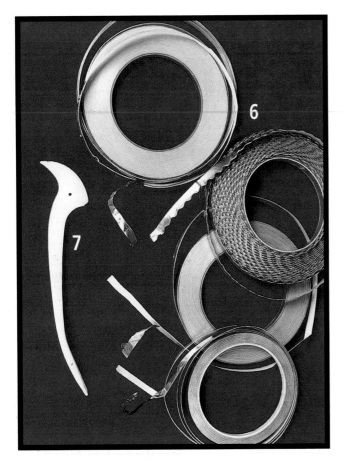

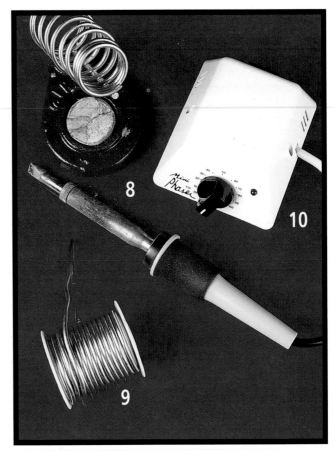

6 Copper Foil

Using copper foil is one of two methods for assembling traditional stained glass projects. Copper foil has an adhesive backing and is used to line the edges of glass. When soldered, the copper foil, along with the solder, holds the glass pieces together. It is available in a variety of widths, decorative edges, and with copper, black, or silver backing.

7 Fid

A fid is used as a burnishing tool when working with copper foil. It is also used to widen the channel in came.

8 Soldering Iron and Stand

A soldering iron is an electric high-temperature iron that is used to melt solder. The stand is a holding device to prevent accidental burns.

9 Solder

Solder is a metal substance purchased on a roll that is melted to create a seam when making "copper foiled" projects. It is also used to seal joints when making "came" projects. The most commonly used types of solder are: 50/50 (50% tin / 50% lead) and 60/40 (60% tin / 40% lead). A nonlead alternative solder is available.

10 Temperature Control

A temperature control is a device that controls the temperature of a soldering iron. Low-wattage soldering irons will need a temperature control to prevent thermo-shocking the glass or melting copper foil and came.

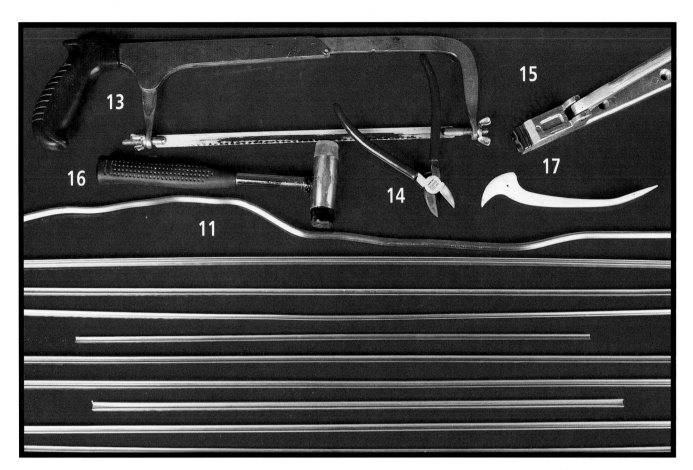

11 Came

Came is lengths of brass, copper, lead, tin, or zinc containing channels in which glass can be inserted. Using came is one of two methods for assembling traditional stained glass projects. "U" came and "H" came are the most commonly used; "U" came allows glass to be inserted into one side, while "H" came allows glass to be inserted into two sides. It is important to know that if lead came is not stretched before it is used, it will sag from the weight of the glass. Came stretchers and came benders are available.

12 Vise (not shown)

A vise can be used to stretch lead came. One end of a length of lead came is clamped into the vise, while a person using grozing pliers clamps down on the other end. The lead came is pulled until it no longer stretches.

13 Hacksaw

A hacksaw is used to cut brass, copper, tin, or zinc came.

14 Lead Dykes

Lead dykes are used to cut lead came.

15 Notching Tool

A notching tool is used to cut precise 45° angles in $\frac{1}{8}$" brass, copper, lead, tin, or zinc "U" came, which create 90° angles when bent.

16 Stained Glass Hammer

A stained glass hammer is a double-headed, soft hammer used to tap glass into a came channel.

17 Fid

A fid is used to widen the channel in came, however, a fid is primarily used as a burnishing tool when working with copper foil.

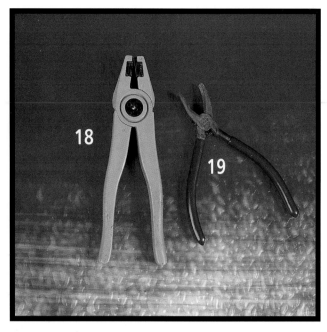

20 Foil Shears

Foil shears are scissors that are used for cutting out patterns when making a copper foil project. They cut out a space between each pattern piece to compensate for the width of the foil. Foil shears are important when exact measurements are required as in a window, door, or premade frame.

21 Lead Shears

Lead shears are scissors that are used for cutting out patterns when making a came project. They cut out a space between each pattern piece to compensate for the width of the came. Lead shears are important when exact measurements are required as in a window, door, or premade frame.

18 Running Pliers

Running pliers are used to run a straight or slightly curved "score" (scratch) line on glass.

19 Grozing Pliers

Grozing pliers are used to break out sharp curves or small pieces of glass.

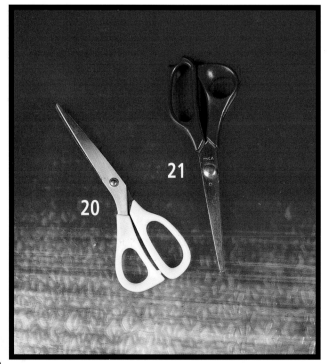

22 Spray Adhesive

Spray adhesive is used to adhere the paper patterns for copper foil or came projects onto the glass prior to the glass pieces being cut out.

23 Flux Brush

A flux brush is a small brush that is used to apply paste or liquid flux.

24 Flux

Flux is an acid-based paste (or liquid) that is used to thoroughly clean a surface to be soldered. Two formulas are shown — 24a is paste flux; 24b is liquid flux. Paste flux is recommended because it does not run off the project nor dry out as quickly as liquid flux. After soldering, flux residue can be thoroughly cleaned off the project with flux/patina remover or glass cleaner.

25 Etching Cream

Etching cream is an acid-based cream that dissolves layers of glass.

26 Finishing Compound

Finishing compound is a polishing compound that is used for stained glass.

27 Stained Glass Putty / Cement

Stained glass putty and cement are substances that are pushed into came channels to prevent the movement of the glass in the came channel and to prevent air and moisture from leaking from a window or door.

28 Patina

Patina is a chemical that changes the color of lead, zinc, or solder into a variety of colors. Lead and/or solder and zinc require two different types of patina to achieve the same color. The two formulas are shown — 28a is patina for zinc; 28b is patina for solder. After using patina, excess patina should be thoroughly cleaned off the project with patina/flux remover or glass cleaner.

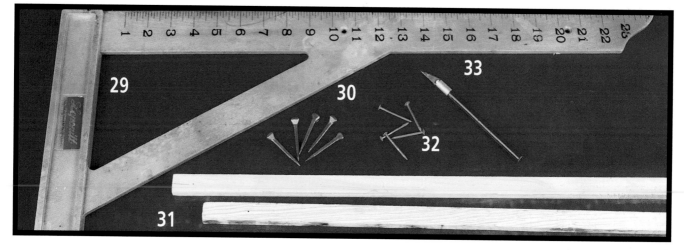

29 L-square

An L-square is a carpenter's tool used to square out the layout board and to "score" (scratch) straight lines.

30 Horseshoe Nails

Horseshoe nails are flat-sided nails that are used to hold glass pieces or came in place.

31 Wood Strips

Wood strips are nailed alongside the squared out area on the layout board. The glass pieces and came frame are lodged against the wood strips to ensure the project maintains straight, squared lines.

32 Nails

Nails are used to attach the wood strips to the layout board.

33 Craft Knife

A craft knife is used to cut detailed patterns on adhesive-backed shelving paper and/or copper foil.

34 Masking Tape (not shown)

Masking tape is used to support pieces of glass when assembling dimensional projects.

35 Particle Board (now shown)

Particle board is used as the layout board in which horseshoe nails can be tacked to hold the project securely in place.

23

Practice Makes Perfect

Before Beginning

1. Before beginning your first stained glass project, it is necessary to practice using various stained glass tools, as well as becoming familiar with the supplies that you will be using. For a complete list, refer to pages 19–23.

2. Clear glass, $1/8$"-thick, is recommended for practice because it is the most inexpensive glass available.

3. Refer back to these basic practice instructions as often as necessary while creating any stained glass project.

Score the Glass

1. Before scoring, make certain there is oil running along the cutting wheel on the glass cutter by gently running it along a piece of paper until a line of oil is visible. If the glass cutter is not self-oiling, dip the head of the cutting wheel in glass-cutting oil.

2. To properly hold the comfort-grip glass cutter, place your thumb on the back side of the cutting wheel and your middle and index fingers on the front, similar to holding a pen or pencil. Your thumb and fingers should be positioned just above the cutting wheel. For extra control, place your free hand in the same position.

3. To properly hold the pistol-grip glass cutter place your thumb on the top of the handle just above the cutting wheel and curl your remaining fingers underneath the handle.

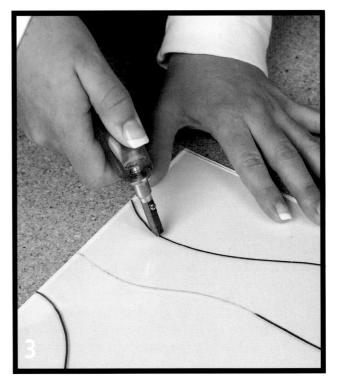

4. To begin scoring with either glass cutter, line up the cutting wheel with the intended score line at a slight downward angle, apply pressure to the cutting wheel, and push away.

5. Stop the score approximately 1/16" before reaching the edge of the glass to prevent damage to the cutting wheel caused by slipping off the edge of the glass. However, if a score is stopped before it is completed, it will be very difficult to line up the cutting wheel with the original score line and the glass will not break properly.

Break the Glass

1. First method: After a score is made, turn the glass over, find the score line, and tap it with the ball end of the glass cutter until a fracture line appears.

   Note: If a score line is visible, but the glass does not fracture or break, this means that not enough pressure was applied to the cutting wheel. However, you cannot score on the same line more than once. Likewise, if tiny chips appear along the score line, too much pressure was applied and the glass may fracture off of the score line. In either case, you will need to start over again.

3. Second method: Running pliers are used to run a straight or slightly curved score line. Line up the line on the top of the running pliers with the beginning of the score line and slightly squeeze the handles.

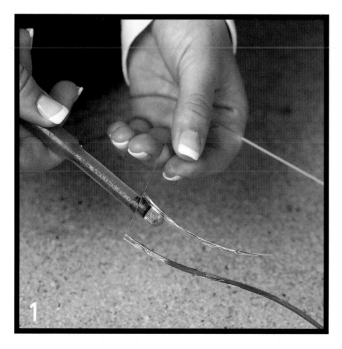

2. Tap and follow the fracture until the line is finished.

4. Third method: Straight or slightly curved lines may also be run by placing your thumbs on either side of the score line and curling your fingers underneath the glass. Using equal amounts of pressure, pry up and out.

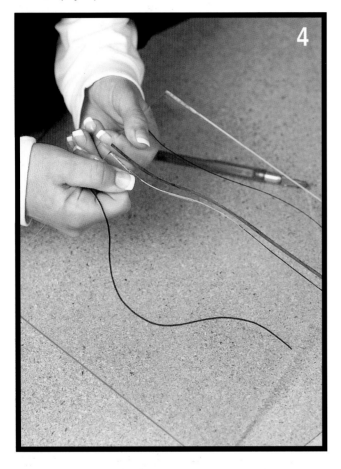

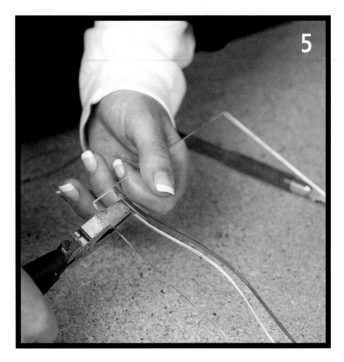

6. Slightly squeeze the handles while prying in a downward and outward motion.

5. Fourth method: Grozing pliers are used to run tight curves and small pieces. Line the head of the grozing pliers to one side of the score line. The curved side of the pliers should always be underneath.

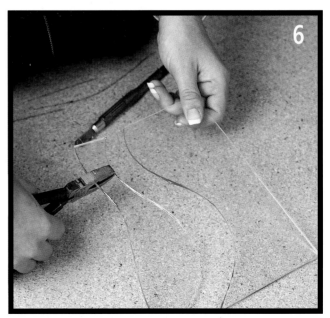

Grind the Glass

1. If the glass of a pattern piece is too big after cutting, grind down the edges to ensure a proper fit.

    Note: When using copper foil, a glass grinder can be used to slightly abrade all the edges of each glass piece to ensure the foil will properly adhere to the glass. Abrading is not required for came projects.

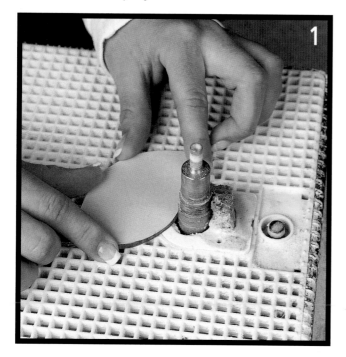

Apply the Copper Foil

1. Before beginning to apply the copper foil, remove the paper pattern, clean the spray adhesive off the glass, and wash any grinding residue from the edges of the glass, otherwise the foil will not adhere properly.

2. Peel off a small amount of the paper backing from the roll of copper foil. Line the ad-

hesive side of the foil on the edge of the glass. Make certain there is an equal amount of foil on either side of the glass. Push the foil down on both sides of the glass, overlapping on the ends.

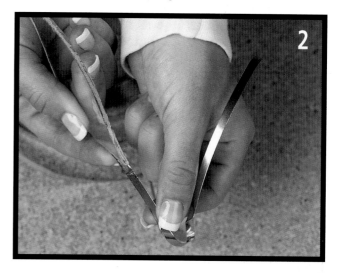

3. Using the flat end of a fid, burnish the foil onto all three sides of the glass.

    Note: Make certain to burnish gently so the foil does not rip.

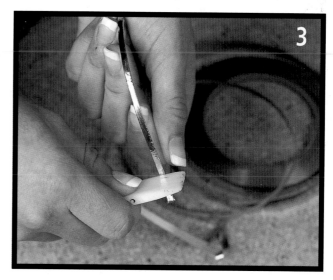

Design Tip: When a foiled project is viewed from a side angle it is sometimes possible to see a double image. Therefore, it is recommended to use copper-backed copper foil when using a copper patina, black-backed copper foil when using a black patina, or silver-backed copper foil when leaving the solder silver.

Stretch and Bend the Lead Came

1. To stretch the lead came, clamp one end of a length of came in a vise. Using grozing pliers, clamp the other end. Pull the came until it will no longer stretch.

   Note: Came stretchers are available, but a vise works just as well.

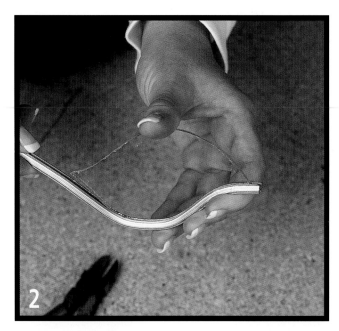

Note: Lead came must be stretched before it is used, otherwise it will sag from the weight of the glass. Brass, copper, tin, and zinc came do not require stretching because they are too rigid.

2. To bend the lead came, insert the edge of the glass piece into the came channel and bend the came by following the contours of the glass piece.

3. To determine where the came should be cut, mark each end at least $1/16$" short of the edge of the glass piece with a permanent marker.

4. Using lead dykes, cut off each end of the came.

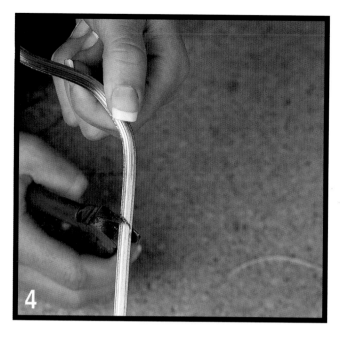

Note: Cutting the came short of the edge of the glass piece prevents the came ends on two pieces of glass from interfering with each other when forming a joint.

Solder the Project

1. When using copper foil, apply paste flux on all exposed copper foil with a flux brush.

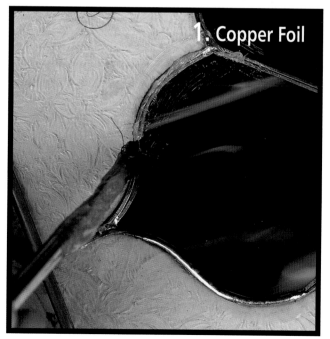

1. Copper Foil

When using came, apply paste flux on all joints with a flux brush.

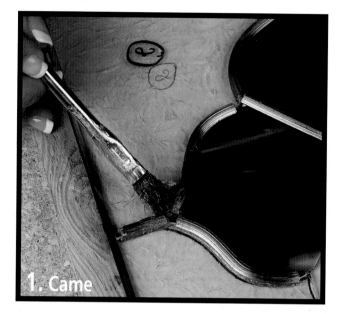

1. Came

2. Straighten a length of solder, but do not cut the length from the roll.

   Note: To properly hold the solder, hold the solder in a gripped fist with the length of solder positioned between two fingers.

   Caution: Be careful to keep the length of solder long enough to prevent burns from heat conducted through the solder and to keep the soldering iron a safe distance away from your skin.

2

3. When using copper foil, touch the tip of the soldering iron to the copper foil at the beginning of the first seam to be soldered. Touch the end of the solder to the tip of the soldering iron. The solder should immediately begin to melt.

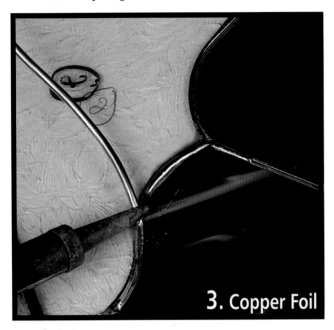

3. Copper Foil

When using came, touch the tip of the soldering iron to the joints to be soldered.

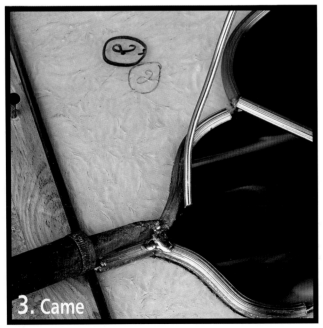

3. Came

4. When using copper foil, slowly drag the soldering iron and solder along the foiled seams. The solder will follow the heat and adhere only to the copper foil. When using came, simply solder each joint.

5. The solder should cool and solidify in a few seconds. If the smoothness of the soldered seam or joint is not satisfactory, reheat the solder by dragging only the soldering iron along the seam or by reheating the solder directly on the joint.

A properly soldered seam should form a small, even mound which provides structural support. A properly tinned seam should form a thin layer of solder onto the copper foil for decorative purposes only.

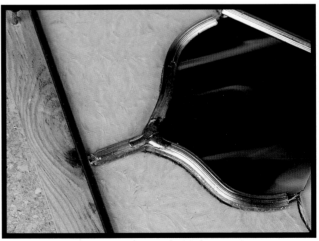

A properly soldered joint should form a small, even mound.

When using copper foil, do not allow the soldering iron to linger in one place for too long or the glass will break from thermoshock. When using came, do not allow the soldering iron to linger in one place for too long or the came will begin to melt.

If tiny holes appear in the solder while soldering, an excess of air or flux is in the seam. This creates bubbles in the solder that burst when cooled. Briefly touch the tip of the soldering iron to these areas until the holes disappear.

6. If the solder is not adhering to the copper foil or came, re-flux the area and try again. When using came, it may be necessary to scrub the joint with steel wool before re-fluxing.

   Note: If an excessive amount of solder builds up in one place, reheat the area and "flick" the solder away. Be very careful as solder can reach temperatures over 300°.

   Do not be alarmed if the solder lands on the glass, it will not cause damage nor will it permanently stick.

When using came, if there are gaps in the joints, the solder will fill them in.

7. Turn the project over. Check for melt-through from the first side. Simply combine it with the new solder.

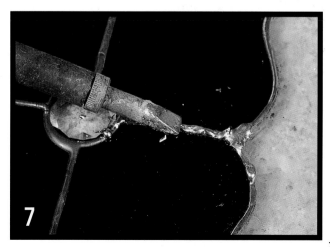

Section 2: *stained glass techniques*

How do I cut glass using a glass cutter?

When beginning any stained glass project, cutting the glass is the most important skill required. This technique could take a lot of practice to master, but the result of your finished piece will depend upon the accuracy of each cut.

1
technique

What You Need To Get Started:

Felt
Glass, opaque to
  color coordinate
  with the colors
  of the frames
Picture frames

Framed Glass Coasters

Approximate size: 4" wide x 6" high

Here's How:

1. Measure the Frame

   1. Using a ruler, measure the inside dimensions of the frame to determine the shape and size of the glass to be cut.

2. Measure the Glass

   1. Measure the glass according to the dimensions of the frame.

   2. Using a permanent marker, mark the glass where it should be cut.

3. Refer back to the following step on pages 24–25 for Practice Makes Perfect:

   Score the Glass
   Note: Use an L-square to score a straight line.

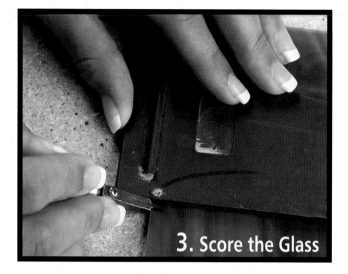

3. Score the Glass

4. Refer back to the following step on pages 25–26 for Practice Makes Perfect:

   Break the Glass

4. Break the Glass

5. Insert the Glass into the Frame

   1. Place the cut glass piece into the frame.

   2. Bend the metal tabs on the back of the frame to hold the cut glass into position.

   3. Adhere felt to the entire back of the frame to prevent the frame from scratching your table.

How do I grind glass using a glass grinder?

What You Need To Get Started:

Glass, clear
Glass epoxy
Glass globs, colored to accent the clear glass

Once the glass for any stained glass project has been cut, grinding is usually the next step. This process is necessary in most cases to ensure that the glass pieces fit properly. It also ensures that the sharp edges are removed from the glass pieces. Grinding is also necessary when using copper foil because the copper foil adheres better to abraded edges. In some rare instances, such as when making stepping stones, grinding should only be done when absolutely necessary.

Coasters with Feet

Approximate sizes: 4" square, 4" x 7" rectangle, 10" x 10" x 10" triangle

Here's How:

1. Refer back to the following step on pages 24–25 for Practice Makes Perfect:

   Score the Glass

1. Score the Glass

2. Refer back to the following step on pages 25–26 for Practice Makes Perfect:

   Break the Glass

2. Break the Glass

3. Grind the Glass

1. Once the glass for the coaster has been broken, it will have sharp edges.

2. Using a glass grinder, slightly grind the edges to eliminate these sharp edges.

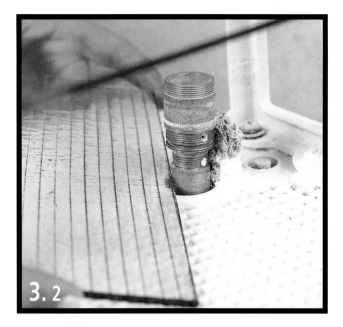

4. Glue the Feet on the Coasters

1. Using a glass epoxy, adhere the glass globs for feet onto one side of the glass.

   Note: When using a textured glass, the glass globs should be adhered to the smooth side.

How do I assemble a stained glass project using copper foil?

There are basically two techniques for assembling a stained glass project. Using copper foil is the first technique that will be detailed for you. This technique is the most popular when working with small, detailed glass pieces because lead came simply cannot bend around the smallest pieces and tends to look too heavy. When copper foil is used as a decorative element, it should be tinned rather than soldered.

3
technique

**What You Need
To Get Started:**

Chain
Clear glass jewel
Copper foil,
  $1/4$" copper backed
Glass: clear gluechip;
  dark green and
  white streakie
Patina, copper
Pattern, 2 copies
Wire, solderable
Wire cutters
Zinc "U" came, $1/8$"

Copper Foil Flower

Approximate size: 12" square

Pattern below.

Here's How:

1. Prepare the Patterns

    1. Using a photocopy machine, enlarge the pattern, and make two copies.

    2. One copy will be the cutout pattern and the other will be the layout pattern. Using a pencil, number each pattern piece (section) on both of the patterns.

Note: Label or color each of the cut-out pattern pieces to correspond with the colors of the chosen glass. If the glass has a pattern, now is the best time to make notes (arrows) to ensure the pattern goes in the same direction throughout the project.

If exact measurements are required, make notes by marking the sizes on the pattern, taking into account the width of the frame.

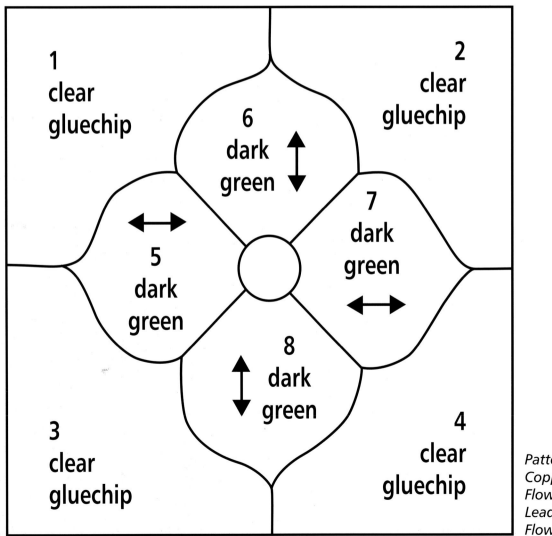

Pattern for Copper Foil Flower and Lead Came Flower

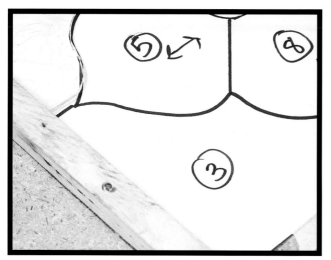

The guidelines on the layout pattern should be traced with a permanent marker to mimic the width of the foiled seams.

2. Estimate the Glass

1. Estimate how much glass is needed for each pattern piece, making certain to allow for possible mistakes.

3. Cut Out the Pattern Pieces

1. Using foil shears, cut out the cutout pattern pieces.

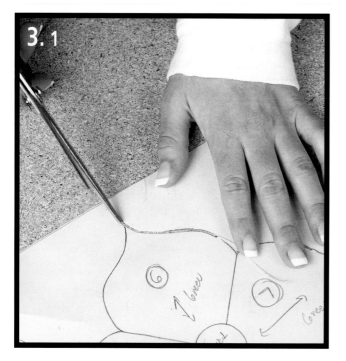

4. Lay Out the Pattern Pieces on the Glass

1. Using spray adhesive, coat the back of each pattern piece.

2. To make scoring easier, place each pattern piece on the smooth side of the corresponding glass.

5. Score, Break, and Grind the Glass

1. Using a glass cutter, score the pattern pieces as close to the paper as possible.

    Note: Avoid scoring on the paper. However, in the event this happens, press a little harder on the glass cutter to cut through the paper and try to finish the line.

2. Completely score and break each piece of glass before moving on to the next.

Note: Do not be concerned if the glass is slightly larger than the pattern. Grinding will ensure a proper fit.

3. Using a glass grinder, grind the glass as necessary.

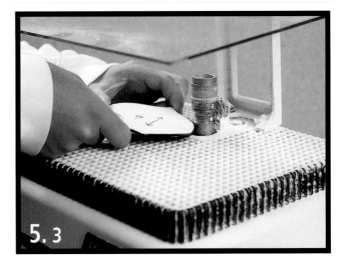

4. Using a grozing stone, slightly abrade the edges of the clear glass jewel.

6. Square Out a Layout Board

1. To help maintain a perfect angle when creating framed projects, a squared layout board is necessary.

2. To make a layout board, cut out a piece of particle board at least two inches larger than your project.

3. Using an L-square, square out a corner on the particle board and mark it with a permanent marker.

4. Using a hammer and nails, attach the wood strips along the edge of the squared corner.

5. Using masking tape, secure the layout pattern onto the layout board, lining up the pattern along the squared corner.

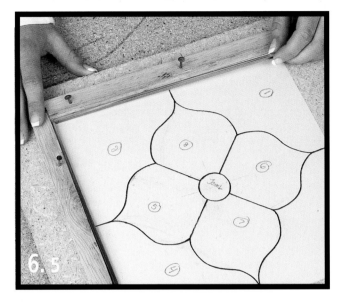

6. To make the frame, measure four lengths of "U" came. Using a hacksaw, cut the came.

7. Lodge two lengths of the came against the squared corner of the layout board as shown in photo 6.5 above.

7. Lay Out the Glass Pieces

1. To ensure a proper fit, lay out the ground glass pieces on the layout pattern, inserting three of the outer glass pieces into the "U" came, and make any adjustments (further grinding or recutting).

   Note: The layout pattern is just a guide. It does not reflect the spaces cut out with the foil shears. It will, however, help detect any large discrepancies in the project.

8. Apply the Copper Foil

Refer back to page 27 for Practice Makes Perfect.

1. Once the glass pieces are fitting properly, remove the paper pattern, clean the spray adhesive off the glass, and wash any grinding residue from the edges of the glass.

2. Using copper foil, line the edges of all the glass pieces, including the clear glass jewel.

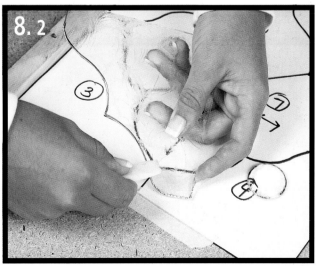

41

3. Using a fid, burnish the foil as necessary.

4. Lay out the foiled glass pieces on the layout pattern. Make certain to insert the outer glass pieces into the came in the squared corner.

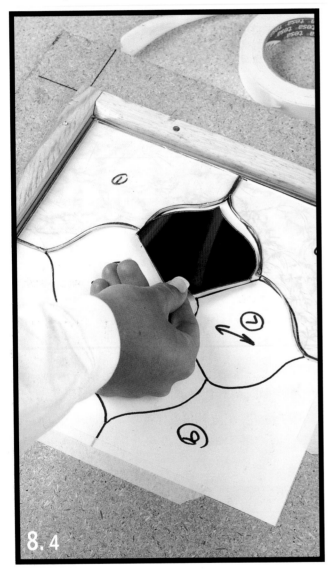

8.4

5. To complete the frame, insert the two remaining lengths of "U" came onto the opposite corner of the project. Using horseshoe nails, tack alongside the outer pieces of "U" came to hold the project securely in place.

9. Tack-solder the Joints

1. Using a soldering iron, melt a bead of solder onto all joints. This will prevent the pieces from moving around while fluxing and soldering.

9.1

10. Solder the Project

Refer back to pages 29–31 for Practice Makes Perfect.

1. Using a flux brush, apply paste flux on all exposed copper foil, including the areas where the seams and the came intersect.

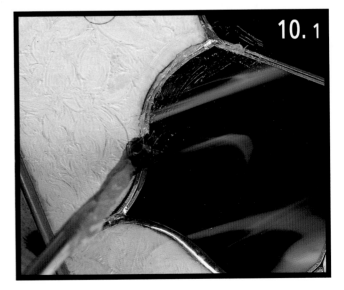

10.1

2. Touch the tip of the soldering iron to the copper foil at the beginning of the first seam to be soldered. Touch the end of the solder to the tip of the soldering iron. The solder should immediately begin to melt.

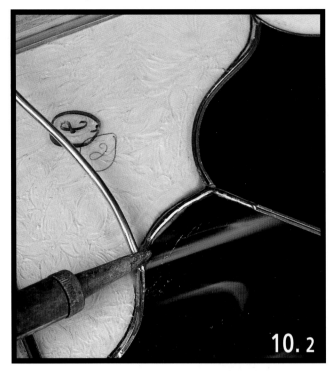

10. 2

3. Slowly drag the soldering iron and solder along the foiled seams. The solder will follow the heat and adhere only to the copper foil.

4. The solder should cool and solidify in a few seconds. If the smoothness of the soldered seam is not satisfactory, reheat the solder by dragging only the soldering iron along the seam again.

5. If the solder is not adhering to the copper foil, re-flux the area and try again.

6. To strengthen the frame, solder the came frame to the soldered seam by extending the soldered seam onto the came.

7. Flux and solder each joint of the "U" came. If there are gaps in the joints, the solder will fill them in.

8. After all seams and "U" came are soldered, remove the horseshoe nails and turn the project over.

   Note: If the project is small, horseshoe nails may be needed to keep it from moving around. The weight of larger projects eliminates this movement.

9. Check for melt-through from the first side. Simply combine it with the new solder.

10. Flux and solder all the seams and joints.

11. Make the Hanger

   1. To make an eyelet, wrap a length of solderable wire around a pencil. Using wire cutters, cut off the excess wire and dip one end of the wire into paste flux.

11. 1

2. At the top of the project, flux one corner where two sections of came have been soldered. This is the strongest area of the frame.

3. Using grozing pliers, hold the eyelet, as it will become extremely hot, and solder one eyelet onto each corner.

4. To hang the stained glass project, cut a length of chain and attach an end to each eyelet.

12. Polish the Project

1. Using glass cleaner, thoroughly clean the project.

2. Patina the seams and frame.

Note: If the zinc came does not change color properly or the patina seems to wipe off easily, clean and scrub the came with steel wool, then reapply the patina.

3. Using a damp cloth, lightly wipe the project to remove excess patina from the glass.

4. Apply a smooth, even coat of finishing compound over the entire project.

5. Allow the finishing compound to dry to a white haze and polish with a clean, dry cloth.

How do I assemble a stained glass project using lead came?

Now that you've tried assembling a stained glass project using copper foil, try assembling one using lead came. Using lead came might seem more difficult because of the stretching process, but you will find that once the came has been stretched and placed around the edges of the glass pieces, the soldering is much easier.

4
technique

What You Need To Get Started:

Clear glass jewel
Glass: clear gluechip; dark green and white streakie
Lead "H" came, 1/4"
Pattern, 2 copies
Steel wool, if needed
Zinc "U" came, 1/8"

Lead Came Flower

Approximate size: 12" square

Pattern on page 38.

Here's How:

1. Refer back to the following steps on pages 38–41 for Technique 3:

   Prepare the Patterns

   Estimate the Glass

   Cut Out the Pattern Pieces
   Note: Lead shears must be used instead of foil shears.

   Lay Out the Pattern Pieces on the Glass

   Score, Break, and Grind the Glass

   Square Out a Layout Board

2. Lay Out the Glass Pieces

   1. To ensure a proper fit, lay out the ground glass pieces on the layout pattern, inserting three of the outer glass pieces into the "U" came, and make any adjustments (further grinding or recutting).

   2. Lay out the inner glass pieces with a slight space between each approximately the width of the "H" came.

      Note: The layout pattern is just a guide. It does not reflect the spaces cut out with the lead shears. It will, however, help detect any large discrepancies in the project.

3. Stretch and Bend the Lead Came

   Refer back to pages 28–29 for Practice Makes Perfect.

4. Assemble the Glass with Lead Came

   1. Select the corner glass piece that corresponds with the squared corner of the layout board and insert it into the "U" came.

2. Measure, bend, and cut the "H" came only to the part of the glass piece that faces the inside of the project, then insert the precut and bent "H" came onto the inner edge of the glass piece.

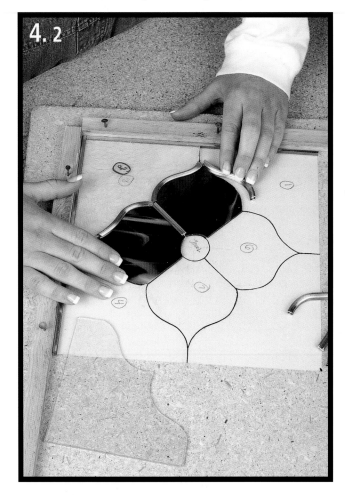

3. Select the next glass piece — either next to or above the previous glass piece. Insert this glass piece into the came of the previously cut piece. Make note of which edges on this glass piece will need came.

4. Repeat Step 3 for each glass piece.

   Note: Assemble the glass pieces from the corner outward in a fan pattern, stopping frequently to verify measurements.

Do not be alarmed if there are gaps in the joints of the "H" came as they will be filled in during the soldering process.

If one or more glass pieces do not seem to be fitting properly, lightly tap the came into place with the rubber end of a stained glass hammer to move the came and glass into position. If this does not work, make any adjustments (further grinding or recutting) to ensure a proper fit.

During the assembly process, the glass has a tendency to come out of the "H" came. To prevent this from happening, tack a horseshoe nail against the came of the last glass pieces to be put in place.

If a glass piece needs to be left partially assembled in order to assemble another area, nail a small scrap of came against the piece to hold it in place. This is necessary when working on large projects. Do not use a horseshoe nail by itself as it may chip the edge of the glass.

Sometimes a glass piece seems to be inserted into the came, but is actually laying underneath the came. Attach any tacky substance (such as tape or wax) to the eraser end of a pencil and lift the glass up and back into the came channel.

5. To complete the frame, insert the two remaining lengths of "U" came onto the opposite corner of the project. Using horseshoe nails, tack alongside the outer pieces of "U" came to hold the project securely in place.

5. Solder the Project

Refer back to pages 29–31 for Practice Makes Perfect.

1. Using a flux brush, apply paste flux on all joints, including the point where the "H" came and the "U" came intersect.

5.1

2. Touch the tip of the soldering iron to the joints to be soldered. Touch the end of the solder to the tip of the soldering iron. The solder should immediately begin to melt.

3. The solder should cool and solidify in a few seconds. If the smoothness of the soldered joint is not satisfactory, reheat the solder on the joint again.

   Caution: Do not allow the soldering iron to linger in one place for too long or the came will begin to melt.

4. Solder all of the joints until they are completely fused.

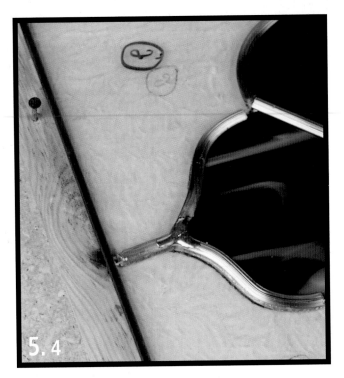

5. If the solder is not adhering to the lead came, re-flux the area and try again or scrub the joint with steel wool before re-fluxing.

6. Flux and solder each joint of the "U" came. If there are gaps in the joints, the solder will fill them in.

7. After all joints are soldered, remove the horseshoe nails and turn the project over.

   Note: If the project is small, horseshoe nails may be needed to keep it from moving around. The weight of larger projects eliminates this movement.

8. Check for melt-through from the first side. Simply combine it with the new solder.

9. Flux and solder all the joints.

6. Refer back to the following step on page 44 for Technique 3:

Polish the Project

How do I etch glass using etching cream?

Etching is a beautiful way to accent glass. This technique is one that allows a single piece of glass to be transformed into an elegant work of art without any assembly as is necessary when using copper foil and/or lead came techniques. Glass etching patterns range from simple monograms to detailed designs.

5
technique

What You Need To Get Started:

Chain
Copper foil,
  ripple-edged,
  ¹/₄" copper backed
Glass: clear bevel,
  6" round
Pattern
Shelving paper,
  adhesive-backed
Transfer paper
Wire cutters

Etched Flower and Butterfly

Approximate size: 6" diameter

Pattern at right.

Here's How:

1. Mask the Glass

   1. Using shelving paper, completely cover the side of the glass that will be etched. In this case, the flat side of the bevel.

*Pattern for
Etched Flower
and Butterfly*

2. Transfer and Cut Out the Pattern Pieces

   1. Using transfer paper, transfer the pattern onto the shelving paper.

   2. Using a sharp craft knife, cut around each pattern piece, leaving a thin line of shelving paper between each

pattern piece. Otherwise the pattern pieces will not be defined as separate areas of the pattern.

Note: Completely cut out and remove the shelving paper for each pattern piece before moving on to the next. This will help guide the line between each piece.

2. Using a damp cloth, lightly wipe the project to remove excess etching cream from the glass.

3. Apply the Etching Cream

   1. Using a flux brush, apply a thick even layer of etching cream to all the exposed areas of the glass.

4. Remove the Etching Cream

   1. After a minimum of 15 minutes, scrape the remaining etching cream back into the jar; it can be reused.

3. Rinse any remaining etching cream residue from the project with water.

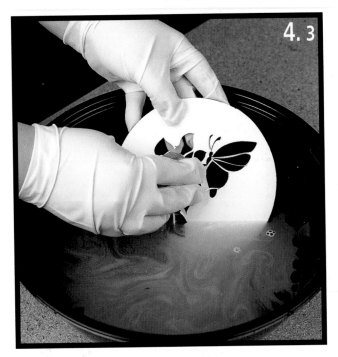

4. Remove the remaining shelving paper from the glass and thoroughly wash the project.

5. Once the glass has dried, the etching should appear frosty white. If there are any irregularities in the etching, the cream was not applied thick enough or was removed too early. If this is the case, remask and recut these areas and repeat the process.

5. Apply the Copper Foil

Refer back to page 27 for Practice Makes Perfect.

1. Using a grozing stone, abrade the edge of the glass bevel. Using copper foil, line the edge.

2. Using a fid, burnish the foil as necessary.

    Note: The copper foil will only withstand the weight of small glass pieces or glass bevels. For larger projects, using "U" came would be more suitable.

6. Refer back to the following step on pages 42–43 for Technique 3:

    Solder the Project
    Note: Before beginning, cover the etched areas of the project with shelving paper to protect them from being stained by the flux or patina. Clean off flux and any patina residue before removing the shelving paper from the etching.

7. Make the Hanger

    1. To hang the stained glass project, cut a length of chain and solder it directly to the frame at two points.

8. Refer back to the following step on page 44 for Technique 3:

    Polish the Project
    Note: Do not use finishing compound on etched projects as it will stain the etching.

Design Tip: Clear glass is most commonly used for etching, but some colored glass can be used.

6
technique

**What You Need
To Get Started:**

Chain
Copper foil,
   ¹/₄" copper backed
Glass: light green
   waterglass; pale
   purple waterglass
Glass paint:
   dark green,
   purple, and red
Paintbrush(es)
Particle board
Patina, copper
Pattern, 2 copies
Wire cutters

How do I paint glass
using glass paint?

Painting on glass is an old art form that can add detail which is not possible otherwise. Today there are several glass paints available in a myriad of colors.

Painted Pansy

Approximate size: 6" wide x 8" high

Pattern at right.

Here's How:

1. Refer back to the following steps on pages 38–40 for Technique 3:

   Prepare the Patterns

   Estimate the Glass

   Cut Out the Pattern Pieces

   Lay Out the Pattern Pieces on the Glass

   Score, Break, and Grind the Glass

2. Paint the Glass

   1. Once the glass pieces are fitting properly, remove the paper pattern, clean the spray adhesive off the glass, and wash any grinding residue from the edges of the glass.

   2. Using a paintbrush and glass paint, paint the freeform design directly onto the glass.

Pattern for Painted Pansy

3. Refer back to the following steps on pages 41–43 for Technique 3:

   Lay Out the Glass Pieces

   Apply the Copper Foil

   Tack-solder the Joints
   Note: Tack alongside the perimeter with horseshoe nails to hold the project securely in place.

   Solder the Project
   Caution: Some glass paints will blister while soldering. In this case, all painting should be completed after the project is assembled.

4. Refer back to the following step on page 52 for Technique 5:

   Make the Hanger
   Note: Solder the chain directly to two joints.

5. Refer back to the following step on page 44 for Technique 3:

   Polish the Project

Design Tip: If using a pattern for painting, tape the pattern onto the particle board. Lay the glass pieces over the pattern and paint. If using opaque glass, a light table is necessary.

7
technique

**What You Need
To Get Started:**

Circle cutter
Drill
Glass, yellow
 waterglass
Lead "H" came,
 ³⁄₁₆"
Vise
Wire (thick),
 solderable
Wire (thin),
 solderable
Wire cutters

How do I cut glass using a circle cutter?

Cutting glass into the shape of a circle is not as hard as it may seem, especially when using a circle cutter. The most critical part is cutting the break lines that extend toward the outer edges of the glass. These lines allow for a controlled breakage.

Wire Flower

Shown on page 32.

Approximate overall size: 18" diameter

Flower center approximate size: 8" diameter

Here's How:

1. Score, Break, and
   Grind the Glass Circles

   1. Using a circle cutter, apply constant pressure to the center and slowly score the circle, moving the cutting wheel with your free hand.

Note: Make certain to apply an adequate amount of pressure to the cutting wheel.

2. Turn the glass over then lightly tap the scored circle until it has completely run.

   Caution: Do not attempt to remove the circle.

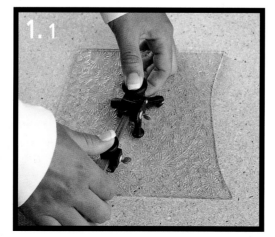

3. Turn the glass over again. Starting at the edge of the circle and working toward the outer edge of the glass, score all of the break lines with a glass cutter.

4. Turn the glass over again and run the break lines. After all lines are run, remove each section of glass one at a time and repeat until the circle is free.

2. Wrap the Lead Came

1. Stretch the lead came. Wrap the glass circles (flower centers) with the lead came and solder the ends together.

   Note: If the center of the flower is over 8" in diameter, the lead might have a tendency to stretch where the stem is attached. In this case, zinc came is recommended.

3. Make the Stem

1. Clamp the ends of two lengths of thick solderable wire into a vise. Insert the other ends into the head of a drill and tighten.

2. Pull the trigger on the drill until the wire is twisted.

   Caution: Be careful removing the twisted wire as it heats up during the twisting process.

4. Make the Flower Petals and Leaves

1. For each flower petal, wrap a length of thin solderable wire around a cylindrical object, such as a bottle, and cut off any excess.

   Note: Making the petals is not an exact science, so experiment with a few to determine the size desired.

2. For each leaf, bend a length of thin solderable wire into leaf shapes and cut off any excess.

5. Solder the Stem and Flower Petals to the Flower Center

1. Solder the stem and the flower petals to one side of the lead came.

6. Solder the Leaves to the Stem

1. Solder the leaves to the back side of the stem.

technique

8

**What You Need
To Get Started:**

Carbon paper
Cardboard
Flat stick
Glass: green and
    yellow streakie;
    purple and
    white streakie;
    white
Pattern
Silicone adhesive,
    clear
Stepping stone,
    premade
Tile grout,
    light gray
Tile grout sealer

How do I assemble
a stained glass project
using tile grout?

There are basically two techniques for making
a stepping stone with a face that resembles stained glass.
Using tile grout is the first technique that will be detailed
for you. The tile grout mimics a soldered seam or came
joint. Tile grout can also be purchased in a variety of
colors.

Tulip Stepping Stone

Approximate size: 12" diameter

Pattern on page 61.

Here's How:

1. Prepare the Pattern
   1. Using a photocopy machine, enlarge the pattern.

      Note: Make certain the pattern comes in at least ⅛" from the outer edge to prevent exposing the edges of the glass when it is grouted.

   2. Lay a piece of carbon paper face down on the stepping stone, then place the pattern on top of the carbon paper.

   3. Using a pencil, trace the pattern.

2. Refer back to the following step on page 39 for Technique 3:

   Estimate the Glass

3. Cut Out the Pattern Pieces
   1. Using lead shears, cut out the pattern pieces.

4. Refer back to the following steps on pages 39–40 for Technique 3:

   Lay Out the Pattern Pieces on the Glass

   Score and Break the Glass
   Note: Make certain the glass is not larger than the pattern because a lot of grinding is not recommended. The grinding marks will show up as rough areas in the grout.

5. Lay Out the Glass Pieces
   1. To ensure a proper fit, lay out the cut glass pieces on the stepping stone and make any adjustments (grinding as little as possible or recutting).

   2. Once the glass pieces are fitting properly, remove the paper pattern and clean the spray adhesive off the glass.

   3. Using a permanent marker, number the cleaned glass pieces to correspond with the transferred pattern. Mark only the sides that will face up when the project is completed.

6. Adhere the Glass Pieces to the Stepping Stone

   Note: Clear silicone adhesive is recommended when the glass is slightly transparent.

   Caution: Make certain to check the label on the silicone adhesive to determine if the stone should be sealed prior to applying the silicone adhesive.

1. Apply a moderate amount of clear silicone adhesive on the back of a glass piece.

7. Grout the Glass Pieces

   1. Using glass cleaner, remove the permanent marker from the glass.

   2. Mix the tile grout according to the package instructions until it is the consistency of batter.

2. Using your finger, smooth the adhesive over the glass, being careful to thin out the adhesive around the edges to prevent it from oozing over the sides when pressed onto the stone.

3. Gently press the glass piece onto the corresponding area of the stepping stone. Repeat the process until the pattern is completed.

4. After two to three hours, test the glass pieces by gently trying to move them. They should be completely secure on the stepping stone.

3. Pour a generous amount of the grout over the stepping stone.

7.3

4. Work the grout in between all the crevices between the glass pieces.

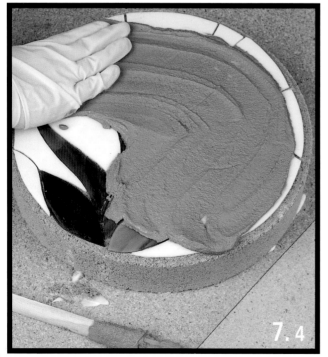

7.4

5. Work the grout around the outer edges of the stepping stone.

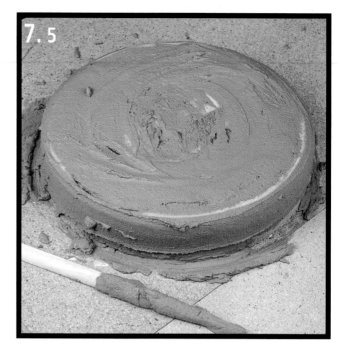

7.5

6. Using a flat stick, scrape off the excess grout.

7. Using a damp cloth, gently wipe the excess grout from the top of the stepping stone.

7.7

8. Using a small piece of cardboard, smooth and round the grout along the outer edges of the stepping stone to blend in with the stone.

7.8

9. Using a damp cloth, gently wipe away all remaining grout from the glass.

7.9

10. Allow the grout to dry for 72 hours before sealing with tile grout sealer.

Caution: This style of stepping stone should be brought indoors where harsh winters occur.

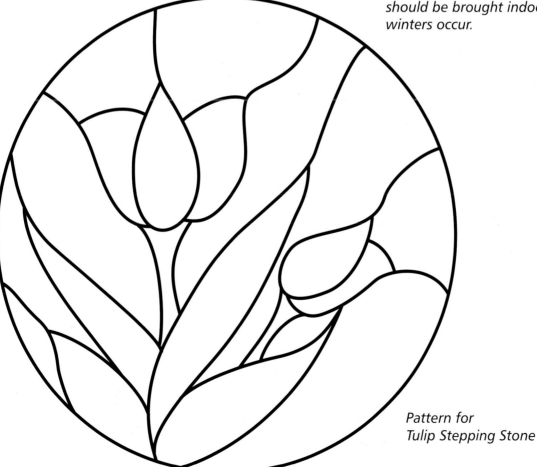

*Pattern for
Tulip Stepping Stone*

technique

9

What You Need To Get Started:

Cement
Cement sealer
Cement topping mix
Chicken wire
Glass: orange with
    white and yellow
    streakie; white with
    light blue streakie;
    yellow with white
    streakie
Pattern, 2 copies
Petroleum jelly
Shelving paper,
    adhesive-backed,
    clear
Stepping stone mold
Wire cutters

How do I assemble a stained glass project using cement?

Now that you've made a stained glass stepping stone using grout, try making one using cement. Both techniques are unique, but render similar results. Stepping stones made with cement weather extremely well and are highly recommended for use in a favorite garden location. Your neighbors will be envious!

Sunburst Stepping Stone

Approximate size: 14" diameter

Pattern on page 67.

Here's How:

1. Select the Mold

   Note: Stepping stone molds come in a variety of shapes and sizes and can be purchased at stained glass supply stores. Garden centers carry a similar version, but they are often flimsy and too shallow.

   There are premade patterns available to fit most stepping stone molds. If other patterns are desired, make a paper template of the inside of the mold to use as a guide for the pattern and reduce or increase the pattern to size. To ensure a proper fit, leave approximately 1/8" clearance from the edge of the mold.

2. Refer back to the following steps on pages 38–40 for Technique 3:

   Prepare the Pattern

   Estimate the Glass

   Cut Out the Pattern Pieces

   Lay Out the Pattern Pieces on the Glass

   Score and Break the Glass
   Caution: Make certain the glass is not larger than the pattern because a lot of grinding is not recommended. The grinding marks will show up as rough areas in the cement topping mix.

3. Lay Out the Glass Pieces

   1. To ensure a proper fit, lay out the cut glass pieces on the layout pattern and make any adjustments (grinding as little as possible or recutting).

   2. Once the glass pieces are fitting properly, remove the paper pattern and clean the spray adhesive off the glass.

3. Using a permanent marker, number the cleaned glass pieces to correspond with the transferred pattern. Mark only the sides that will face up when the project is completed.

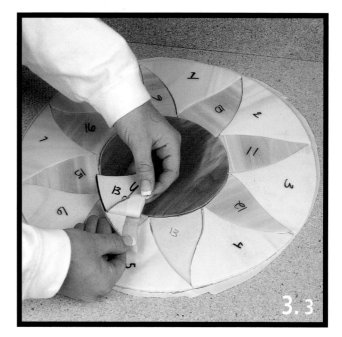

4. Cut a piece of clear shelving paper slightly larger than the mold. Peel off the paper backing and carefully place the shelving paper over the glass pieces.

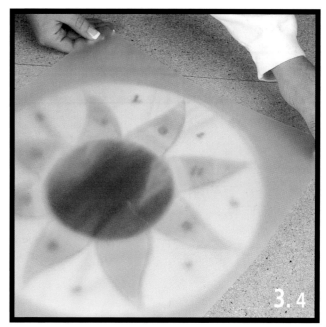

5. Once all the glass pieces are secure, gently smooth the shelving paper.

   Note: If there are any wrinkles in the shelving paper, these areas will be noticeably different in the cement.

6. Using a sharp craft knife, trim off the excess shelving paper so the glass pieces will fit inside the mold.

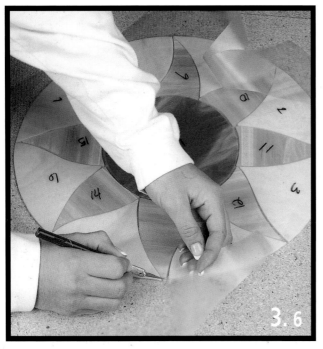

7. Turn the glass pieces over, glass side up.

4. Prepare the Chicken Wire

1. Using wire cutters, cut the chicken wire to the shape of the mold approximately $^1/_2$" to $^3/_4$" smaller than the mold to prevent the wire from sticking out of the finished stepping stone.

2. Set the chicken wire aside.

5. Prepare the Mold

1. Using a clean cloth, apply a thin layer of petroleum jelly to the inside of the mold.

2. Carefully lay the shelving paper (with the glass facing up) on the bottom of the mold.

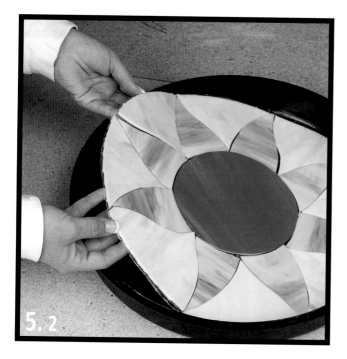

2. Pour the cement topping mix over the glass pieces at the bottom of the mold until the mold is approximately $1/4$ full.

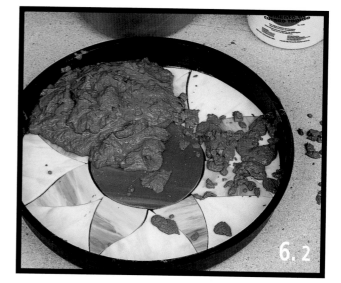

6. Mix and Pour the Cement Topping Mix

Note: If quick-set cement topping mix and/or cement are used, mix both at the same time.

1. Mix a moderate amount of cement topping mix according to the package instructions.

3. Smooth the cement topping mix until it appears even.

7. Mix and Pour the Cement

1. Mix a generous amount of cement according to the package instructions.

2. Pour the cement over the cement topping mix until the mold is approximately $1/2$ full.

3. Smooth the cement until it appears even.

4. Flatten out and place the precut chicken wire on top of the cement.

6. Smooth the cement until it appears even.

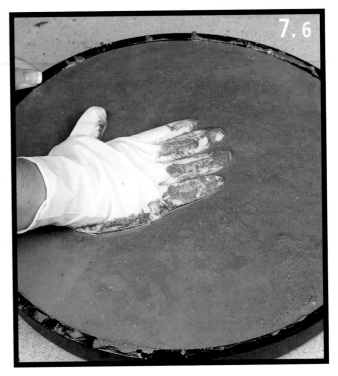

5. Pour the remainder of the cement over the chicken wire until the mold is full.

8. Work Out the Air Bubbles

1. Using a stained glass hammer, gently tap the underside of the table directly underneath the mold and around the mold on the surface of the table. This will work out the air bubbles and excess water.

2. Soak up the excess water on the surface of the cement with paper towels.

3. Repeat the process until all excess water has been absorbed.

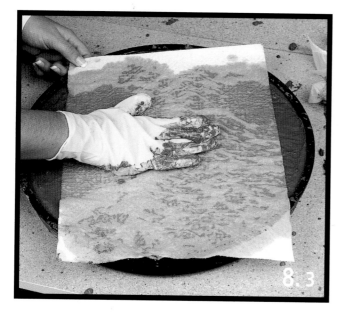

9. Allow the Cement to Set Up

1. Do not move the mold until it has set up. Quick-set cement will set up in approximately two to three hours; regular cement requires one to two days.

2. When set up, remove the stepping stone from the mold and remove the shelving paper.

3. Mix more cement topping mix to fill in any cracks or bubbles that may appear in the cured topping mix.

4. Using glass cleaner, remove the permanent marker from the glass.

5. After 30 days, seal with a cement sealer.

Caution: This style of stepping stone should be brought indoors where harsh winters occur.

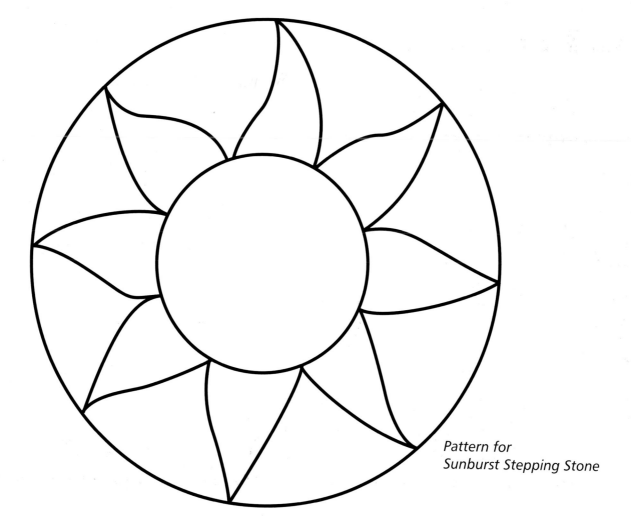

Pattern for Sunburst Stepping Stone

Section 3: *projects beyond the basics*

How do I make a stained glass project using a single bevel?

Bevels are available in a myriad of shapes and are available in several thicknesses. Most often bevels are used in the center of stained glass projects as the focal point, but many times they are etched.

Small Etched Diamond Bevel

Approximate size: 4" wide x 7" high

Pattern at right.

Here's How:

1. Refer back to the following steps on pages 50–52 for Technique 5:

   Mask the Glass

   Transfer and Cut Out the Pattern Pieces

   Apply the Etching Cream

   Remove the Etching Cream

   Apply the Copper Foil

2. Refer back to the following steps on pages 42–44 for Technique 3:

   Solder the Project
   Note: Before beginning, cover the etched areas of the project with shelving paper to protect them from being stained by the flux or patina. Clean off flux and any patina residue before removing the shelving paper from the etching.

   Make the Hanger
   Note: Ribbon is used instead of a chain.

   Polish the Project
   Note: Do not use finishing compound on etched projects as it will stain the etching.

What You Need To Get Started:

Copper foil, ripple-edged, ¼" copper backed
Glass: clear bevel, 3" x 5" diamond
Patina, black
Pattern
Ribbon
Shelving paper, adhesive-backed
Wire, solderable
Wire cutters

Pattern for Small Etched Diamond Bevel

2
project

**What You Need
To Get Started:**

Bevels (4)
Copper foil,
  3/16" black backed
Monofilament line
Patina, black
Wire
Wire cutters

How do I make
a stained glass project
using more than one bevel?

Using more than one bevel in a stained glass project allows you to create several cluster combinations. Experiment with bevels to see what creations can be made. Depending on the number of bevels being used and their varying angles, soldering is recommended to fill in the gaps where the intersecting bevels are not exact.

Beveled Star Cluster

Approximate size:
4" wide x 5¹/₂" high

Here's How:

1. Refer back to the following steps on pages 41–44 for Technique 3:

   Lay Out the Glass Pieces

   Apply the Copper Foil
   Note: Using a grozing stone, slightly abrade the edges of the bevels before applying the copper foil.

   Tack-solder the Joints
   Note: Tack alongside the perimeter with horseshoe nails to hold the project securely in place.

   Solder the Project

   Make the Hanger
   Note: Monofilament line is used instead of a chain.

   Polish the Project

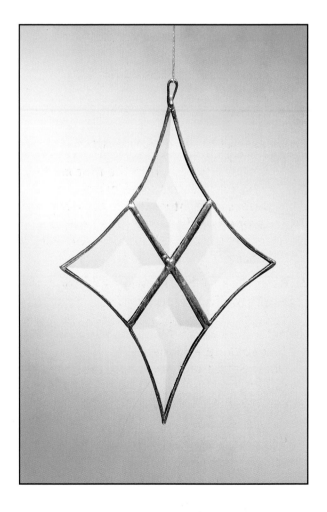

How do I make a three-dimensional box using bevels?

What You Need To Get Started:

Bevels, 2" x 2" (4)
Copper foil,
   $^7/_{32}$" copper backed
Mirror, $^1/_8$"
Patina, copper

Dimensional objects can be made using bevels, but bevels are not necessary. Any glass can be cut and used. Bevels, however, add a special touch to such creations and give them a timeless look. As an alternative, try using a mirror as the back of the box (instead of as the bottom) so whatever is displayed inside will be reflected.

Beveled Box

Approximate size: 2" square

Here's How:

1. Score, Break, and Grind the Mirror

   1. Cut a 2" square from the mirror. *Caution: Always score mirror on the mirror side, otherwise it will not break properly. When grinding mirror, be extremely careful not to disturb the silver backing.*

2. Refer back to the following steps on pages 41–44 for Technique 3:

   Apply the Copper Foil

   Tack-solder the Joints
   Note: Before tack-soldering, tape the sides together to form right angles, avoiding the corners. After tack-soldering the corners, remove the tape. Tack-solder the bottom in the same manner.

   Solder the Project
   Note: Tin the outer seams thicker than usual.

   Polish the Project

4
project

**What You Need
To Get Started:**

Chain
Copper foil,
  3/16" silver backed
Glass, white
  iridescent
Pattern,
  2 copies
Peak bevels,
  clear,
  1" x 1" (3)
Wire cutters
Zinc "U" came,
  3/16"

How do I cut glass
from a pattern with
a curve or an angle?

Glass can be cut into virtually any shape. Cutting glass on a curve or at an angle is more difficult than cutting straight lines. Cutting glass into simple shapes, with only slight curves or angles, is recommended for the first few projects you plan to make as this will give you the "feel" before cutting more difficult shapes.

Moon and Beveled Stars

Approximate size: 5$^{1}/_{2}$" wide x 9" high

Pattern at right.

Here's How:

1. Refer back to the following steps on pages 38–40 for Technique 3:

   Prepare the Pattern

   Cut Out the Pattern Pieces

   Lay Out the Pattern Pieces on the Glass

   Score, Break, and Grind the Glass

2. Refer back to the following step on page 46 for Technique 4:

   Lay Out the Glass Pieces

3. Assemble the Moon with Zinc Came

   1. Gently bend the zinc came around the moon.

4. Refer back to the following step on pages 47–48 for Technique 4:

   Solder the Joints
   Note: Tack the came in place with horseshoe nails.

5. Refer back to the following step on pages 41–42 for Technique 3:

   Apply the Copper Foil Around the Peak Bevels

6. Tin the Peak Bevels

   1. Tin the outer edges of the peak bevels.

7. Refer back to the following step on page 52 for Technique 5:

   Make the Hanger
   Note: Solder the chain directly to the moon and the peak bevels.

8. Refer back to the following step on page 44 for Technique 3:

   Polish the Project

Pattern for Moon and Beveled Stars

Copper foil,
   $^3/_{16}$" black backed
Glass: dark green
   transparent;
   medium blue
   waterglass
Nightlight
Nightlight base clip
Patina, black
Pattern, 2 copies

How do I cut glass
from a pattern with
a severe curve or angle?

There are glass saws available that cut glass at very sharp angles, but stress fractures can become a problem and future breakage could be the result. Stress fractures can occur at the highest point of any curve. To prevent stress fractures when cutting glass with intense curves or sharp angles, it is best to cut the glass in small sections. If sharp curves or angles are used in a larger project, break lines will be needed.

Fleur de Lis Nightlight

*Approximate size:
4" wide x 4" high*

Pattern at right.

Here's How:

1. Refer back to the following steps on pages 38–44 for Technique 3:

   Prepare the Patterns
   Note: The pattern must be small enough that the weight of the glass is in proportion to the size of the nightlight base clip.

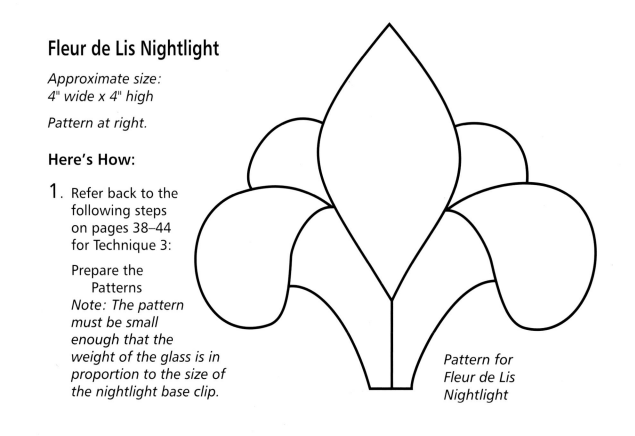

*Pattern for
Fleur de Lis
Nightlight*

Estimate the Glass

Cut Out the Pattern Pieces

Lay Out the Pattern Pieces on the Glass

Score, Break, and Grind the Glass

Lay Out the Glass Pieces

Apply the Copper Foil

Tack-solder the Joints
Note: Tack alongside the perimeter with horseshoe nails to hold the project securely in place.

Solder the Project

Polish the Project

2. Solder the Project to the Base Clip

   1. Solder the stained glass project to the front of the base clip on the front facing bar.

   2. Remove any excess metal from the base clip.

3. Attach the Nightlight

   1. Clip the stained glass base clip to the nightlight.

6
project

How do I incorporate glass globs into my stained glass project?

**What You Need
To Get Started:**

Chain
Glass: amber;
  white; green
  gluechip
Glass globs,
  red (3)
Lead "U" came,
  $^3/_{32}$"
Pattern, 2 copies
Wire cutters

Glass globs are a wonderful addition to any stained glass project. They are round or slightly oblong in shape, and come in an enormous range of colors, including opaque, translucent, and varying shades of each color. Because glass globs can also be found in a wide range of sizes, they are a simple and popular way to add berries, bubbles, and flower centers to your creation.

Christmas Candle and Holly

Approximate size:
5$^1/_4$" wide x 11$^1/_2$" high

Pattern at right.

Here's How:

1. Refer back to the following steps on pages 38–40 for Technique 3:

   Prepare the Patterns

   Estimate the Glass

   Cut Out the
      Pattern Pieces

   Lay Out the Pattern
      Pieces on the Glass

   Score, Break, and
      Grind the Glass

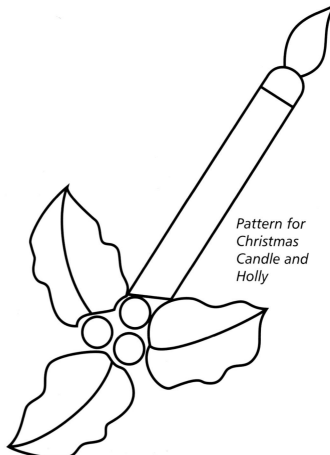

Pattern for Christmas Candle and Holly

2. Refer back to the
following steps on
pages 46–48 for
Technique 4:

Lay Out the
Glass Pieces

Stretch the
Lead Came

Assemble the Glass
with Lead Came

Solder the Project
*Note: Tape can be
used instead of
horseshoe nails
when using thin
came, but it is
recommended to
tack along the peri-
meter with horse-
shoe nails.*

3. Refer back to the
following step
on page 52 for
Technique 5:

Make the Hanger
*Note: Solder the
chain directly to
two joints.*

4. Refer back to the
following step
on page 44 for
Technique 3:

Polish the Project

project

What You Need To Get Started:

Copper foil,
  7/32" black backed
Glass, light green
  waterglass
Glass globs:
  dark purple (9);
  light purple (6)
Pattern,
  2 copies
Patina, black
Wire, solderable
Wire cutters

How do I use glass globs to create an entire stained glass project?

The combination of several glass globs as the exclusive source of glass for a stained glass project is a unique way to add dimension. Most often, glass globs are used to create clusters, such as berries or flowers. It is a challenge to solder glass globs together, because they have a tendency to move around easily.

Grape Cluster

Approximate size: 6 1/2" wide x 3" high

Pattern below.

Here's How:

1. Refer back to the following steps on pages 38–44 for Technique 3:

   Prepare the Pattern

   Cut Out the Pattern Piece

   Lay Out the Pattern Piece on the Glass

Score, Break, and Grind the Glass

Lay Out the Glass Pieces
Note: Place the glass globs in a freeform grape cluster.

Apply the Copper Foil
Note: Using a grozing stone, slightly abrade the edges of the glass globs.

Tack-solder the Joints

Solder the Project
Note: Fill in the gaps between the glass globs with solder and tin the outer edges.

Polish the Project

2. Add the Grape Vine

   1. To make the curly grape vine, wind two lengths of solderable wire around a pencil.

   2. Solder each vine onto the top of the grape cluster — one on each side of the leaf.

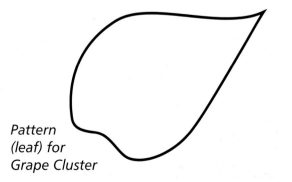

Pattern (leaf) for Grape Cluster

8
project

**What You Need
To Get Started:**

Copper foil,
  $^7/_{32}$" copper backed
Glass: clear gluechip;
  iridescent
Glass globs,
  light blue (3)
Marble, black
Patina, copper
Pattern, 2 copies
Wire (thick
  copper),
  solderable
Wire (thin
  copper),
  solderable
Wire cutters

How do I make
a three-dimensional project
using glass globs?

Dimensional objects can be made using glass globs. Wire is used to hold the glass globs together. The heavier the wire, the more strength and stability the project will have. In this case, wire was also used as the plant stake.

Dragonfly Plant Stake

Approximate size: 6" wide x 3" long

Pattern below.

Here's How:

1. Refer back to the following steps on pages 38–44 for Technique 3:

   Prepare the Patterns

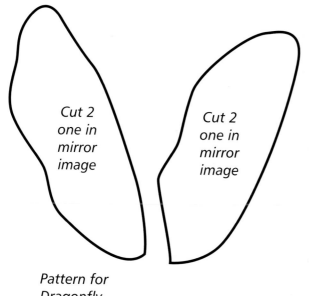

   Pattern for
   Dragonfly
   Plant Stake

   Estimate the Glass

   Cut Out the Pattern Pieces

   Lay Out the Pattern Pieces on the Glass

   Score, Break, and Grind the Glass

   Apply the Copper Foil

   Tack-solder the Joints
   Note: Tack alongside the perimeter of the right set of wings with horseshoe nails to hold the wings securely in place. Repeat the process for the left set of wings.

   Solder the Project

   Polish the Project

2. Make the Head and Body of the Dragonfly

   1. Wrap thin solderable wire around the black marble to make the head.

   2. Wrap thin solderable wire around each of the light blue glass globs to make the body.

   3. Using wire cutters, cut off the excess wire.

   4. Solder the head and body together, wire to wire.

   5. Solder the wings to the wire on both sides of the body between the first and second glass globs.

   6. Make the antennae from the thin wire and solder to the top of the head.

3. Make the Plant Stake

   1. Cut a length of thick solderable wire to make the plant stake.

   2. Bend a portion of the wire the same length as the body of the dragonfly.

   3. Solder the bent portion of the wire to the underside of the body.

9

project

What You Need To Get Started:

Beads
Copper foil,
   $^3/_{16}$" copper backed
Glass, amber and
   white streakie
Mirror, $^1/_8$"
Patina, copper
Pattern, 2 copies
Wire (thin
   copper),
   solderable
Wire cutters

How do I use beads to accent the solderable wire on my stained glass project?

Decorative beads are a popular design element in several art forms. Likewise, beads can be used to accent stained glass projects. Beads can be threaded onto wire to be used as an accent or as a handle. Also, beads can be glued with glass epoxy to the bottom of any vase or bowl to serve as feet.

Beaded Vase

Approximate size: 5" wide x 5" high

Pattern at right.

Here's How:

1. Refer back to the following steps on pages 38–40 for Technique 3:

   Prepare the Pattern

   Estimate the Glass

   Cut Out the Pattern Pieces

   Lay Out the Pattern Pieces on the Glass

   Score, Break, and Grind the Glass

2. Score, Break, and Grind the Mirror

   1. Cut the bottom from the mirror.
      Note: The sides of this vase angle inward toward the bottom. The best way to

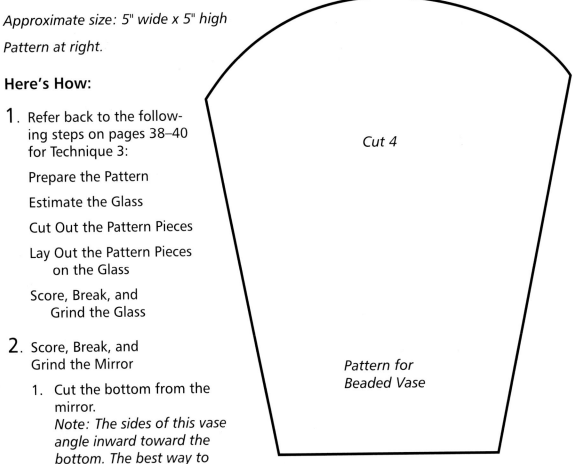

Cut 4

Pattern for Beaded Vase

determine the size of the mirrored bottom is to tack solder all the sides together, then place the vase upright on a piece of mirror and mark an outline on the mirror from the inside of the vase.

Caution: Always score mirror on the mirror side, otherwise it will not break properly. When grinding mirror, be extremely careful not to disturb the silver backing.

3. Refer back to the following steps on pages 41–43 for Technique 3:

   Apply the Copper Foil

   Tack-solder the Joints
   Note: Before tack-soldering, tape the sides together at the appropriate angles, avoiding the corners. After tack-soldering the corners, remove the tape. Tack-solder the bottom in the same manner.

   Solder the Project
   Note: Tin the outer seams.

4. Add Beads onto the Copper Wire

   1. Cut a length of solderable copper wire and thread beads onto it as desired.

5. Solder the Copper Wire onto the Vase

   1. Bend the copper wire into any decorative shape and solder onto the vase at the soldered seams.

6. Refer back to the following step on page 44 for Technique 3:

   Polish the Project

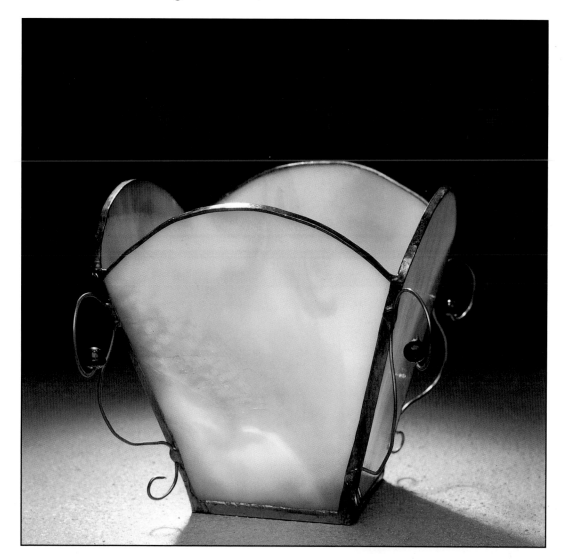

10
project

Copper foil,
    $1/4$" copper backed
Glass, amber and
    white streakie
Mirror, $1/8$"
Patina, copper
Patterns, 2 copies
Wire (thick
    copper),
    solderable
Wire (thin
    copper),
    solderable
Wire cutters

How do I use solderable wire to hang my stained glass project?

Solderable wire can serve many purposes when working with stained glass. In this application, the wire serves as the hanging device for this stained glass wall sconce. The wire can be bent and shaped to enhance the styling of the project. If desired, beads can be added to accent the wire as described in Project 9 on pages 82–83.

Triangular Wall Sconce

Approximate size: 6" wide x 9" high

Patterns at right and on page 85.

Here's How:

1. Refer back to the following steps on pages 38–44 for Technique 3:

   Prepare the Patterns

   Estimate the Glass

   Cut Out the Pattern Pieces

   Lay Out the Pattern Pieces
       on the Glass

   Score, Break, and Grind the Glass

   Apply the Copper Foil

   Tack-solder the Joints
   Note: Before tack-soldering, tape the sides together at the appropriate angles, avoiding the corners. After tack-soldering the corners, remove the tape.

   Solder the Project

   Polish the Project

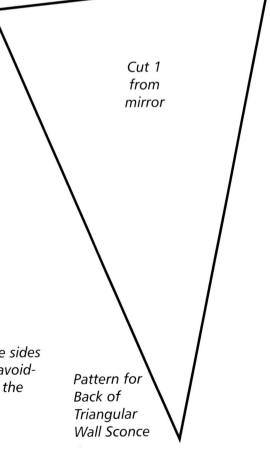

Cut 1
from
mirror

*Pattern for
Back of
Triangular
Wall Sconce*

2. Make the Hanger

1. Cut a length of thick solderable wire and solder it directly to two joints.

2. Twist the wire at the top to make a loop for hanging.

3. Bend the Wire

1. Cut lengths of thin solderable wire and bend them into any decorative shape, such as curly-cues.

2. Solder the wires onto the sconce along the soldered seams, at the top of each side, and at the top of the hanger.

3. Reinforce the solder at the points where the wire is attached to the sconce.

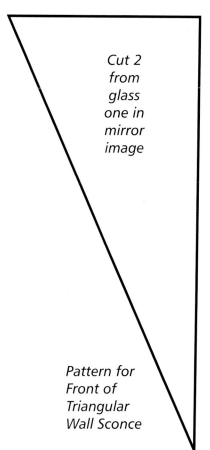

Cut 2 from glass one in mirror image

Pattern for Front of Triangular Wall Sconce

11
project

What You Need To Get Started:

Bevels, 1" x 5" (2)
Copper foil,
   ¼" black backed
Glass, clear
Leaves, dried
Mirror, ⅛"
Patina, black
Raffia
Ribbon
Wire (thick
   copper),
   solderable
Wire cutters

How do I place a flat object in between a double pane of glass ?

When choosing objects to be positioned between the glass panes, anything from dried flowers and leaves to pieces of vintage lace to heirloom photos can be used.

Dried Leaf Wall Sconce

Approximate size:
11" wide x 5" high x 3" deep

Here's How:

1. Refer back to the following steps on pages 39–40 for Technique 3:

   Estimate the Glass
   Note: Selecting the thinnest glass and mirror possible is recommended so the project does not look too bulky.

   Score, Break, and
      Grind the Glass
   Note: Cut ten 3" x 5" rectangles out of the clear glass.

2. Score, Break, and Grind the Mirror
   Note: Cut one 5" x 11" rectangle out of the mirror for the back of the wall sconce. Cut one 3" x 11" rectangle out of the mirror for the bottom of the wall sconce.

   Caution: Always score mirror on the mirror side, otherwise it will not break properly. When grinding mirror, be extremely careful not to disturb the silver backing.

3. Lay Out the Leaves

   Note: Using a grozing stone, slightly abrade the edges of the glass before laying out the leaves.

   1. Using a small amount of spray adhesive, tack the dried leaves in place on five of the clear glass pieces.

   2. Sandwich the dried leaves with five of the remaining clear glass pieces.

4. Apply the Copper Foil

   1. Line the edges of the five glass pieces with leaves, the bevels, and the mirror with copper foil.

      Caution: Make certain to completely seal the sandwiched glass together so the solder will not ooze in between the two pieces of glass.

5. Lay Out the Glass Pieces

   1. Lay out the sandwiched glass rectangles and bevels on a squared layout board in the following order: rectangle, bevel, rectangle, bevel, rectangle.

   2. The remaining two sandwiched glass pieces will be used for the sides.

6. Refer back to the following steps on pages 42–43 for Technique 3:

Tack-solder the Joints
Note: Before tack-soldering, tape the sides together to form right angles, avoiding the corners. After tack-soldering the corners, remove the tape. Tack-solder the bottom in the same manner.

Solder the Project
Note: Solder the rectangles and bevels together. Tin the outer seams.

7. Refer back to the following step on page 52 for Technique 5:

Make the Hanger
Note: Bend a length of thick, solderable wire into a squared "U" shape instead of using chain. Solder the ends of the wire to the full length of the sides for added strength. Wrap the wire with ribbon and add raffia.

8. Refer back to the following step on page 44 for Technique 3:

Polish the Project

12
project

Bevels: 1" x 1" (6);
   1" x 5" (2);
   1" x 10" (4)
Glass: clear;
   light amber
   waterglass;
   olive green
   transparent
Patina, black
Zinc "U" came,
   1/8"
Zinc "H" came,
   flat, 3/16"

How do I suspend the bottom of a stained glass tower to serve as a platform for a votive candle?

Towers are a unique way to add subtle lighting by using either a votive candle or a tea light. The bottom can be placed at the actual bottom of the tower or suspended. This particular votive tower is made using a geometric design.

Bevel Votive Tower

Approximate size: 2" wide x 10" high

Here's How:

1. Refer back to the following steps on pages 39–41 for Technique 3:

   Estimate the Glass

   Score, Break, and Grind the Glass
   Note: Because this is a freeform pattern, lay out the bevels first, then measure and cut the glass.

   The clear glass used to hold the votive will not be a perfect square due to the width of the "U" came which makes two sides of the tower wider. In this case approximately 1/2". A perfect square can be accomplished by subtracting the width of the "U" came.

   Square Out a Layout Board

2. Refer back to the following steps on pages 46–48 for Technique 4:

   Assemble the Glass with
      Zinc Came
   Note: The zinc came can be pre-cut or cut while assembling the project. Each side of the tower should be assembled vertically from left to right as a separate project.

   Solder the Project
   Note: To suspend the platform, solder the glass platform to one of the sides, then assemble each additional side around the platform. Before soldering the last side of the tower, clean the inside of the tower.

3. Refer back to the following step on page 44 for Technique 3:

   Polish the Project

13
project

**What You Need
To Get Started:**

Copper foil,
  $^7/_{32}$" black backed
Glass: dark green
  and white streakie;
  medium amber
  and white streakie;
  solid white
Grinder bit, $^1/_8$"
Lightswitch cover
Patina, black
Pattern, 2 copies
Zinc "U" came, $^1/_8$"

How do I
drill holes in glass?

Anytime the surface of glass is manipulated, the chance for
fracturing or breaking exists. When drilling holes in glass, a
light, even pressure and a constant supply of water should be
applied during the drilling process.

Geometric Lightswitch Cover

Approximate size: 3" wide x 8" high

Pattern below.

Here's How:

1. Refer back to the following steps on pages 38–40 for Technique 3:

   Prepare the Patterns
   Note: Use a lightswitch cover as a template for the approximate size and position of the screw holes. Also remember to leave an open area in the middle for the actual switch.

   Estimate the Glass

   Cut Out the Pattern Pieces

   Lay Out the Pattern Pieces on the Glass

   Score, Break, and Grind the Glass

2. Drill the Holes

   1. Using a grinder with the appropriate-sized grinder bit, drill the holes for the screws.

3. Refer back to the following steps on pages 41–43 for Technique 3:

   Lay Out the Glass Pieces

   Apply the Copper Foil

   Tack-solder the Joints
   Note: Tack alongside the perimeter with horseshoe nails to hold the project securely in place.

   Solder the Project

4. Frame the Project

   1. To make the frame, measure the lengths of "U" came. Using a hacksaw or notching tool, cut the came.

   2. Insert the lengths of came onto the project. Using horseshoe nails, tack alongside the outer pieces of "U" came to hold the project securely in place.

   3. Solder the joints.

5. Refer back to the following step on page 44 for Technique 3:

   Polish the Project

6. Install the Lightswitch Cover

   1. Screw the lightswitch cover to the wall.

      Caution: Make certain you do not tighten the screws too tightly as they could crack the glass.

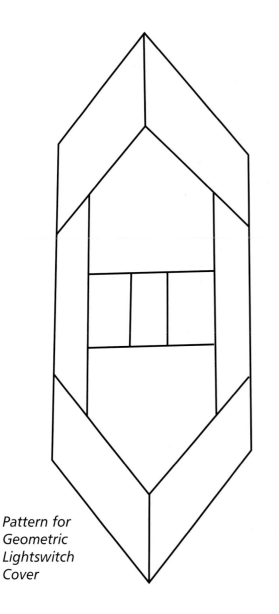

Pattern for Geometric Lightswitch Cover

14
project

What You Need To Get Started:

Chain
Copper foil sheet, adhesive-backed
Glass, cobalt blue, purple, and white streakie
Pattern
Patina, black
Shelving paper, adhesive-backed
Wire cutters
Zinc "U" came, $1/8$"

How do I use solder and copper foil on top of glass as a design element?

Applying soldered copper foil on top of glass is an unusual way to create artwork, but the results can be phenomenal.

Pattern for Filigree Tree

Filigree Tree

Approximate size: 4" wide x 9" high

Pattern at left.

Here's How:

1. Refer back to the following step on page 40 for Technique 3:

   Score, Break, and Grind the Glass

2. Refer back to the following step on page 50 for Technique 5:

   Mask the Glass
   Note: A sheet of copper foil is used instead of shelving paper. Make certain to smooth and burnish the foil onto the glass, taking precaution so it does not rip.

3. Transfer and Cut Out the Pattern Pieces

   1. Adhere the shelving paper onto the sheet of copper foil.

      Note: This prevents the spray adhesive from interfering with the tinning process.

   2. Using spray adhesive, adhere the pattern onto the shelving paper.

3. Using a sharp craft knife, cut around the pattern.

   Note: Make certain to cut through the shelving paper and the copper foil.

4. Remove the background from around the pattern (both the shelving paper and the copper foil) and remove only the shelving paper from the pattern itself. This is a reversed method of the etching projects.

4. Tin the Pattern

   1. Tack alongside the glass piece with horseshoe nails to hold the project securely in place.

   2. Using a flux brush, apply flux to the copper foil.

   3. Tin the copper foil.

      Caution: Tin as quickly as possible to prevent thermoshock, because in this application a greater surface area is being subjected to intense heat.

      Note: For the more confident, mound or make swirls in the solder to create interesting textures.

5. Frame the Project

   1. To make the frame, measure four lengths of "U" came. Using a hacksaw or notching tool, cut the came.

   2. Lodge all four lengths of the came around the glass piece.

   3. Using horseshoe nails, tack alongside the outer pieces of "U" came to hold the project securely in place.

   4. Solder the joints.

6. Clean the Project

   1. Using glass cleaner sprayed lightly onto a cloth, thoroughly clean the project.

      Caution: Take precaution when cleaning so the sharp corners and edges are not disturbed; they will have a tendency to lift.

2. If desired, patina the solder and frame.

3. Using a damp cloth, lightly wipe the project to remove excess patina from the glass.

7. Refer back to the following step on page 52 for Technique 5:

   Make the Hanger
   Note: Solder the chain directly onto the frame.

8. Refer back to the following step on page 44 for Technique 3:

   Polish the Project

93

15
project

What You Need To Get Started:

Bevels, clear*
Glass, clear and
    colored*
Patina, black
Pattern paper
Peak bevels, clear*
Pyramid jewels,
    colored*
Zinc "H" came,
    flat, 3/16"
Zinc "U" came, 1/4"

*The size and
number of bevels,
glass pieces, peak
bevels, and pyramid
jewels depends on
the size of the
window you are
making.*

How do I assemble an entire stained glass window?

Assembling an entire window definitely requires some practice and therefore is not recommended as your first project.

Geometric Window

Approximate size: 24" wide x 36" high

Here's How:

1. Refer back to the following step on page 39 for Technique 3:

   Estimate the Glass

2. Design a Pattern

   1. On a sheet of pattern paper, lay out an assortment of bevels and jewels in a free-form pattern to the size of the window you are making.

      Note: Take into account the extra space that is needed for the "H" and "U" came. There may be areas in the pattern into which a bevel or jewel will not fit.

3. Make a Pattern

   1. After all the bevels and jewels are laid out, trace each piece onto the pattern paper, removing each piece as it is traced. This will leave the areas needed to fill in with clear or colored glass.

4. Refer back to the following steps on pages 40–41 for Technique 3:

   Score, Break, and Grind the Glass
   Note: Cut the clear or colored glass into squares or rectangles that will fill in the spaces around the bevels and jewels.

   Square Out a Layout Board

   Lay Out the Glass Pieces

6. Refer back to the following steps on pages 46–48 for Technique 4:

   Assemble the Glass with Zinc Came
   Note: Assemble the glass pieces in a vertical pattern from left to right, frequently rechecking your measurements. To ensure a proper fit, additional grinding to bevels and jewels may be necessary.

   Solder the Project

7. Install the Window

   1. Refer to Installation below.

Installation

The framework around a preexisting window generally has enough room to add stained glass. However, a ledge of no less than $1/4$" deep is required to properly install stained glass.

When measuring for a square or rectangular window, subtract at least $1/16$" from both the length and the width to ensure a proper fit and to allow for expansion and contraction. When measuring for an oval, circular, octagonal, or other odd-shaped window, make a cardboard template that is slightly smaller than the window.

To install stained glass against an existing window, small nails, caulking, or decorative moulding can be used to hold the art glass in place. To replace an existing window with stained glass, it is highly recommended that a company which installs windows professionally is consulted about proper installation.

16
project

**What You Need
To Get Started:**

Carbon paper
Cardboard
Flat stick
Glass: green with
   yellow streakie;
   royal blue with
   light blue streakie;
   yellow with
   white streakie
Pattern
Silicone adhesive,
   clear
Stepping stone,
   premade
Tile grout,
   light gray
Tile grout sealer

How do I use
colored glass to enhance the
illusion of illumination
on a stepping stone?

Stepping stones are becoming very popular, but would be considered an unusual usage for stained glass because traditional stained glass is illuminated by the light that can be seen through the glass. When glass is placed onto a flat surface where no light can shine through, it would seem obvious that the glass would appear dull. This is not necessarily the case. Using bright colored glass pieces can actually create an optical illusion that light is reflecting back from behind the glass pieces.

Dogwood Stepping Stone

Approximate size: 12" diameter

Pattern below.

Here's How:

1. Refer back to the following steps on page 58 for Technique 8:

   Prepare the Pattern

   Cut Out the Pattern Pieces

2. Refer back to the following steps on pages 39–40 for Technique 3:

   Estimate the Glass

   Lay Out the Pattern Pieces on the Glass

   Score and Break the Glass

3. Refer back to the following steps on pages 58–61 for Technique 8:

   Lay Out the Glass Pieces

   Adhere the Glass Pieces to the Stepping Stone

   Grout the Glass Pieces

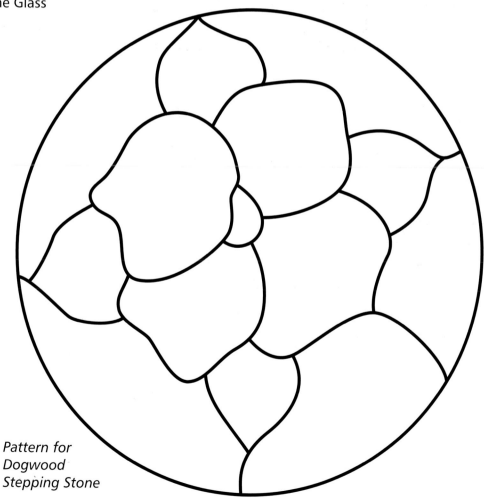

Pattern for Dogwood Stepping Stone

**What You Need
To Get Started:**

Carbon paper
Cardboard
Flat stick
Glass: blue gray and
    white streakie;
    frosted gray;
    light caramel
    streakie
Pattern
Silicone adhesive,
    clear
Stepping stone,
    premade
Tile grout,
    light gray
Tile grout sealer

How do I combine
basic geometric shapes together
to create unique patterns
on a stepping stone?

Traditionally, stepping stones are most often round in shape, however square stepping stones offer a diverse look and alternative. When working with basic geometric shapes, a square is the perfect choice for the base. Imagine the possibilities for patterns using simple, basic geometric shapes — the combinations are virtually endless!

Geometric Stepping Stone

Approximate size: 12" square

Pattern below.

Here's How:

1. Refer back to the following steps on page 58 for Technique 8:

   Prepare the Pattern

   Cut Out the Pattern Pieces

2. Refer back to the following steps on pages 39–40 for Technique 3:

   Estimate the Glass

   Lay Out the Pattern Pieces on the Glass

   Score and Break the Glass

3. Refer back to the following steps on pages 58–61 for Technique 8:

   Lay Out the Glass Pieces

   Adhere the Glass Pieces to the Stepping Stone

   Grout the Glass Pieces

Pattern for Geometric Stepping Stone

18
project

What You Need To Get Started:

Cardboard
Faceted jewels
Geodes
Glass, clear and colored
Glass beads
Polished rocks
Shelving paper, adhesive-backed
Silicone adhesive, clear
Stepping stone, premade
Tile grout, light gray
Tile grout sealer

How do I break a piece of glass and reassemble it to resemble a mosaic?

When one thinks of a mosaic, the use of small mosaic tiles used to decorate floors and walls in European homes and churches comes to mind. In this application, pieces of broken glass, beads, jewels, and polished rocks replace the ceramic tiles.

Mosaic Stepping Stone

Approximate size: 12" square

Here's How:

1. Refer back to the following step on page 39 for Technique 3:

   Estimate the Glass
   Note: Because this is a freeform pattern, additional items such as beads and jewels can be incorporated into the design.

2. Score and Break the Glass

   1. Using shelving paper, completely cover one side of the glass and geode. This will prevent the glass from "flying" everywhere when it is broken.
   Note: If a specific shape is desired, cut the glass into that shape prior to covering it with shelving paper. Once the glass has been broken, it will retain the shape of the shape in which it was cut.

   2. Turn the glass over. Using a glass cutter, score many crisscrossing lines over the glass. Do not be concerned about scoring over another score line; an erratic breaking pattern is what is desired.

   3. Turn the glass back over. Using a stained glass hammer, break the glass into small pieces.

3. Lay Out the Broken Glass

   1. In a freeform pattern, lay out the broken glass pieces on a premade stepping stone. Place beads, jewels, polished rocks, etc., as desired.
   Note: Remove the broken pieces of glass, one at a time, from the piece of shelving paper and place in the same position on the premade stepping stone. It will be similar to putting a puzzle together.

   2. Make a mental note or a sketch of the layout to help remember the placement of the items, then remove them.

4. Adhere the Glass Pieces to the Stepping Stone

   1. Using silicone adhesive, adhere each piece of glass, bead, jewel, or polished rock into position as close as possible to the original layout.

5. Refer back to the following step on pages 59–61 for Technique 8:

   Grout the Glass Pieces
   Note: A toothbrush or soft-bristle brush may be needed to clean the grout from the jewels and rocks.

Design Tip: If an actual pattern is desired, transfer the pattern onto the stepping stone as described on page 58 (Tulip Stepping Stone, Prepare the Pattern).

Section 4: *gallery*

Nancy Sledd and Mary Lu Winger

of Sledd/Winger Glassworks, Richmond, Virginia, discovered the magic of working with flat glass more than two decades ago, and they have never looked back.

Early in their careers, Nancy and Mary Lu made windows and boxes, but later switched to fireplace screens, full-scale room dividers, and freestanding sculptures. With that change, their line eventually grew into limited-edition works with a price range of $1,900 to more than $6,000.

The partners, who are primarily self-taught artists, push beyond the usual limits of stained glass construction to produce innovative architectural works in glass. Their use of highly textured and rare, colorful glass (obtained from sources in the U.S., Europe, and South America) sets Sledd/Winger Glassworks apart in any craft gallery or art exhibition. By utilizing the Tiffany method of construction, the screens are lightweight, durable, and functional in the home.

Sledd/Winger Glassworks is available in craft

galleries and fine furnishings showrooms across the U.S. and is regulary presented at the Baltimore ACC (American Craft Council) Craft Fair, the Philadelphia Buyers Market of American Craft, the Smithsonian Craft Show, and other juried exhibitions.

In addition to their works having been featured in several publications and the recipients of several awards, Sledd/Winger Glassworks is proud to have some of their custom pieces as part of private collections belonging to Jimmy Dean, Stephen King, and Dennis Rodman.

designed by Sledd/Winger Glassworks

designed by Sledd/Winger Glassworks

Judy Apol of Contemporary Glassworks, changed glasswork from an avocation to a vocation at the end of 1981.

Manipulating the elements of shape, color, texture, and light into finished glass pieces — whether they be hangings, lamps, boxes, or freestanding pieces — continues to be an obsession and a joy for Judy.

Judy exhibits in ten to twenty-six retail shows each year in the midwest and eastern U.S. and markets her creations through museum shops, galleries, and other gift shops. Commission work completes her schedule.

Judy is a married grandmother with two sons and resides in Grand Rapids, Michigan.

designed by Judy Apol

designed by Judy Apol

Angelika Traylor

specializes in one-of-a-kind lamps, autonomous panels, and architectural designs.

Her award-winning work can be recognized by its intricate, jewel-like composition and is often referred to as having painterly qualities.

A few of her pieces, shown here, reflect an original and intensive design process, implemented with meticulous craftsmanship and an unusually beautiful selection of glass.

Angelika's work has been featured in many publications and she has been recognized by her inclusion in several *Who's Who* reference books.

Her glasswork is displayed in several private collections in the U.S., Europe, and South America, and in 1993 and 1997 her pieces were chosen to become part of the permanent Christmas Ornament Collection of the White House.

designed by Angelika Traylor

designed by Angelika Traylor

Mike Green has been working in glass since 1974 when he opened his first studio in Ogden, Utah. Since that time, he has produced many commissions in glass, ranging from small residential panels to large architectural and religious installations.

He currently lives and works in Artspace in Salt Lake City, Utah, where he continues to explore new techniques and applications of glass in an environment with artists working in many different mediums.

"Art is important in our everyday lives, and I am interested in finding how the captivating medium of glass can be used to evoke emotion."

designed by Mike Green

Metric Conversions

INCHES TO MILLIMETRES AND CENTIMETRES

MM-Millimetres CM-Centimetres

INCHES	MM	CM	INCHES	CM	INCHES	CM
$1/8$	3	0.9	9	22.9	30	76.2
$1/4$	6	0.6	10	25.4	31	78.7
$3/8$	10	1.0	11	27.9	32	81.3
$1/2$	13	1.3	12	30.5	33	83.8
$5/8$	16	1.6	13	33.0	34	86.4
$3/4$	19	1.9	14	35.6	35	88.9
$7/8$	22	2.2	15	38.1	36	91.4
1	25	2.5	16	40.6	37	94.0
$1 1/4$	32	3.2	17	43.2	38	96.5
$1 1/2$	38	3.8	18	45.7	39	99.1
$1 3/4$	44	4.4	19	48.3	40	101.6
2	51	5.1	20	50.8	41	104.1
$2 1/2$	64	6.4	21	53.3	42	106.7
3	76	7.6	22	55.9	43	109.2
$3 1/2$	89	8.9	23	58.4	44	111.8
4	102	10.2	24	61.0	45	114.3
$4 1/2$	114	11.4	25	63.5	46	116.8
5	127	12.7	26	66.0	47	119.4
6	152	15.2	27	68.6	48	121.9
7	178	17.8	28	71.1	49	124.5
8	203	20.3	29	73.7	50	127.0

YARDS TO METRES

YARDS	METRES	YARDS	METRES	YARDS	METRES	YARDS	METRES	YARDS	METRES
$1/8$	0.11	$2 1/8$	1.94	$4 1/8$	3.77	$6 1/8$	5.60	$8 1/8$	7.43
$1/4$	0.23	$2 1/4$	2.06	$4 1/4$	3.89	$6 1/4$	5.72	$8 1/4$	7.54
$3/8$	0.34	$2 3/8$	2.17	$4 3/8$	4.00	$6 3/8$	5.83	$8 3/8$	7.66
$1/2$	0.46	$2 1/2$	2.29	$4 1/2$	4.11	$6 1/2$	5.94	$8 1/2$	7.77
$5/8$	0.57	$2 5/8$	2.40	$4 5/8$	4.23	$6 5/8$	6.06	$8 5/8$	7.89
$3/4$	0.69	$2 3/4$	2.51	$4 3/4$	4.34	$6 3/4$	6.17	$8 3/4$	8.00
$7/8$	0.80	$2 7/8$	2.63	$4 7/8$	4.46	$6 7/8$	6.29	$8 7/8$	8.12
1	0.91	3	2.74	5	4.57	7	6.40	9	8.23
$1 1/8$	1.03	$3 1/8$	2.86	$5 1/8$	4.69	$7 1/8$	6.52	$9 1/8$	8.34
$1 1/4$	1.14	$3 1/4$	2.97	$5 1/4$	4.80	$7 1/4$	6.63	$9 1/4$	8.46
$1 3/8$	1.26	$3 3/8$	3.09	$5 3/8$	4.91	$7 3/8$	6.74	$9 3/8$	8.57
$1 1/2$	1.37	$3 1/2$	3.20	$5 1/2$	5.03	$7 1/2$	6.86	$9 1/2$	8.69
$1 5/8$	1.49	$3 5/8$	3.31	$5 5/8$	5.14	$7 5/8$	6.97	$9 5/8$	8.80
$1 3/4$	1.60	$3 3/4$	3.43	$5 3/4$	5.26	$7 3/4$	7.09	$9 3/4$	8.92
$1 7/8$	1.71	$3 7/8$	3.54	$5 7/8$	5.37	$7 7/8$	7.20	$9 7/8$	9.03
2	1.83	4	3.66	6	5.49	8	7.32	10	9.14

Index